package and
p.o.p. structures

dhairya

Published by

WWW.INDEXBOOK.COM

Design Contribution: Dhairya

ISBN: 978-84-96309-42-5

If product is the heart, packaging is its public face. Tremendous demands are made of it. Good packaging is supposed to protect during storage and transportation. On the shop shelf, it is supposed to dazzle the audience and seduce a buyer. No wonder, a small fortune is invested to make packaging just about right.

For a dedicated graphic designer, packaging is the heady cocktail of elusive art and perfect science. While the packaging exterior acts as the come-hither eye candy, the dynamically balanced structure preserves and protects.

introduction

Having studied the history of packaging inside out, we have 286 designs those are aesthetically stimulating and structurally, most efficient cocoons.

Each of these designs can be straight off used as templates. Or, for the more demanding designers, spur that wild thought towards a more exhilarating design. Either way, the results will be satisfying.

These 286 designs are for packaging and presentation (Cartons, Display Cartons, Dispensers, Display & POP, Jackets, Files & Folders, Paper Bags etc.). They cover food, cosmetics, toiletries, pharma, and much else!

Besides the book, the attached CD, an e-book in HTML files format, compatible with Internet Explorer 4.0 upward, PDF, Illustrator EPS vector files for Mac & IBM compatibility is the perfect companion for all hard-pressed graphic designers.

CONTENTS

CARTONS 9

DISPLAY CARTONS 133

DISPENSERS 161

DISPLAYS AND P.O.P. 175

JACKETS 245

FILES AND FOLDERS 267

BAGS 293

CARTONS

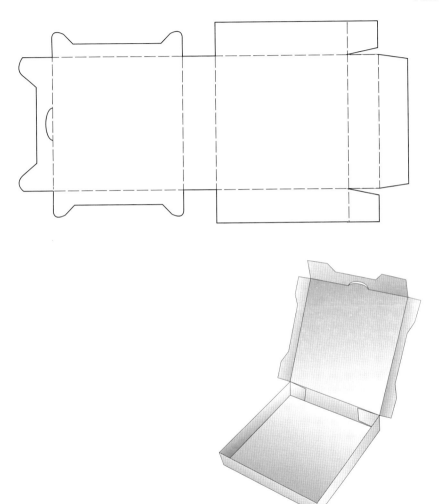

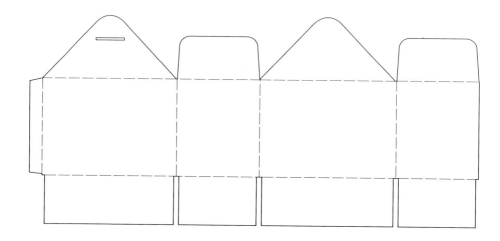

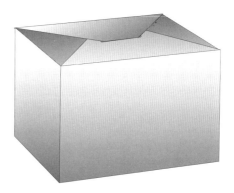

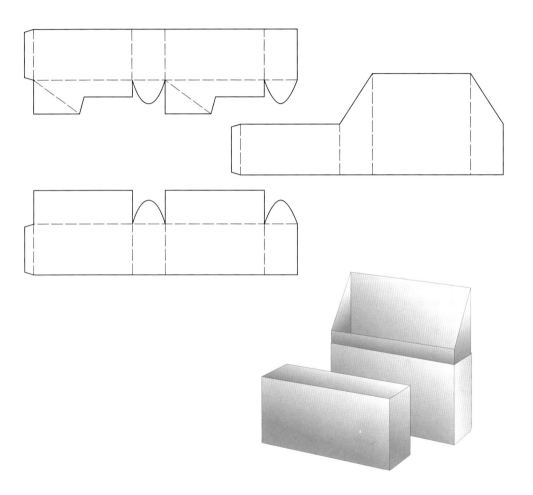

Shoe package

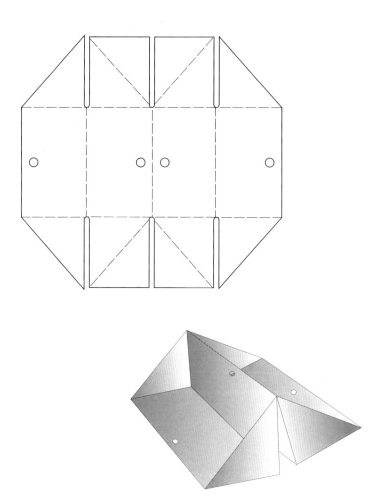

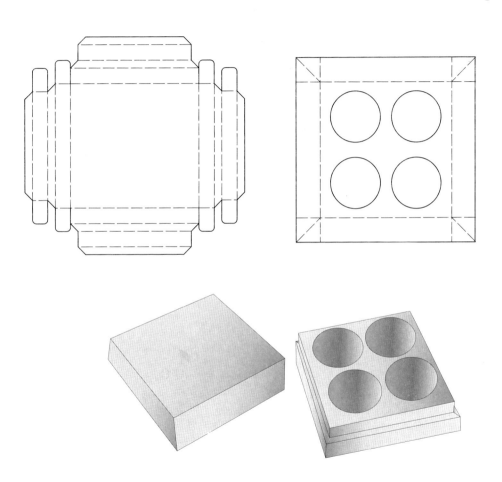

Sleeve and slinding tray package

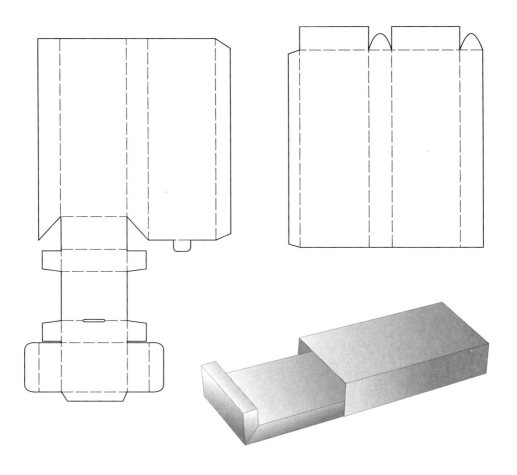

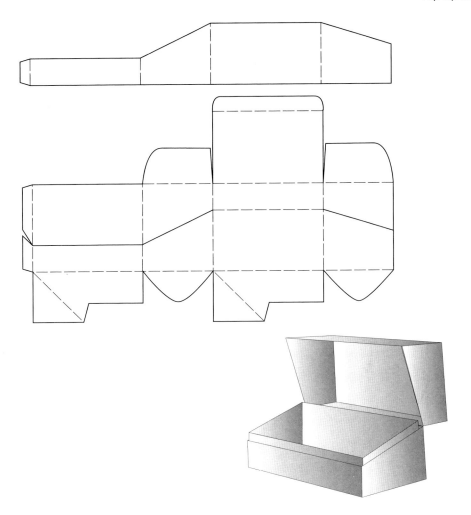

Double wall tray with lid

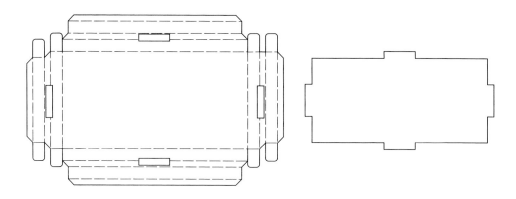

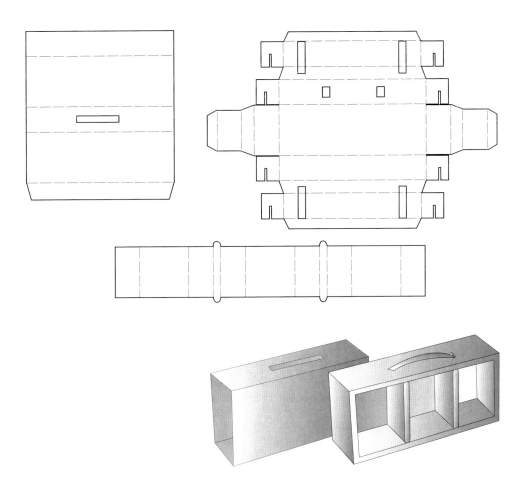

Double wall slinding tray with handle & sleeve

Perforated tear open box

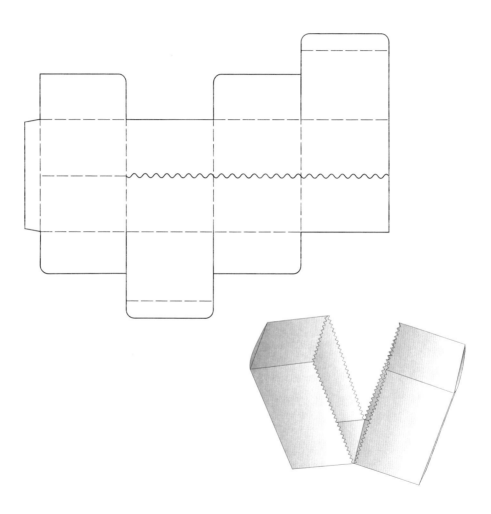

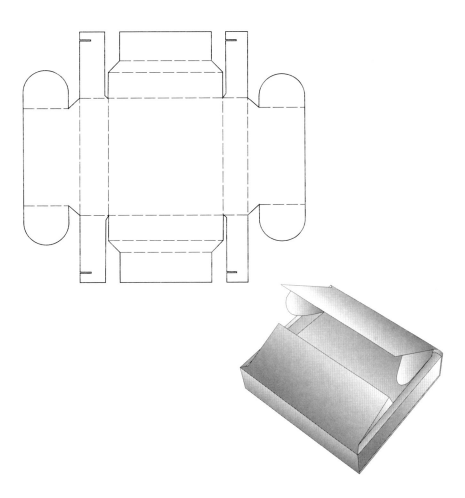

Multi decker tray carton

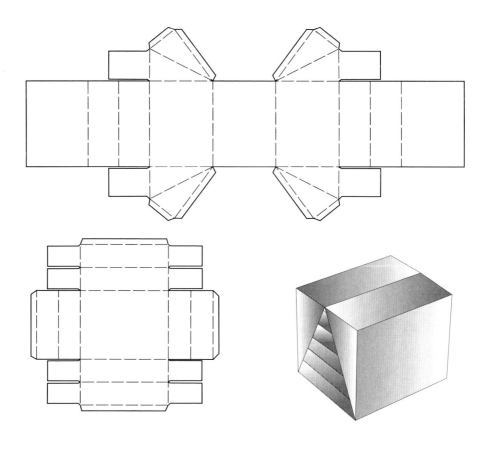

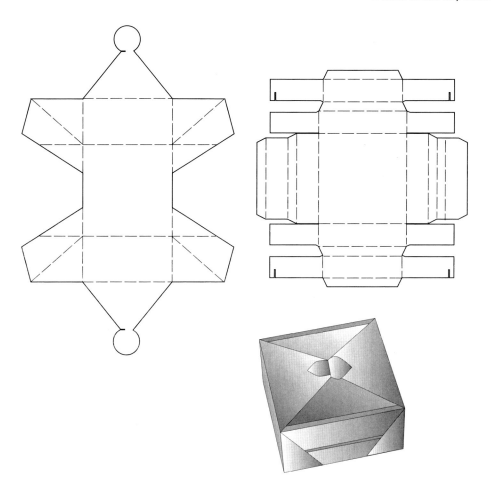

Straight tuck carton with hinged lid and self tray cavity

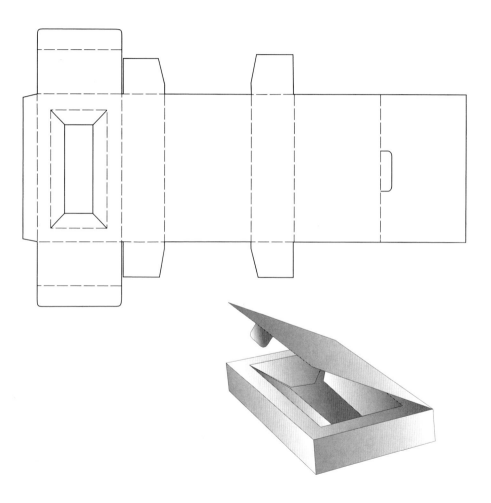

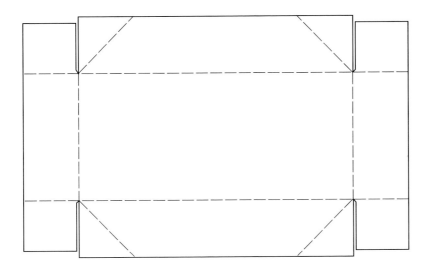

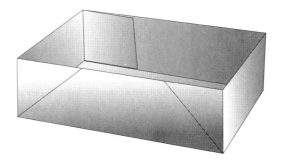

Cartons 23

Auto assemble tray with hinged auto assemble lid

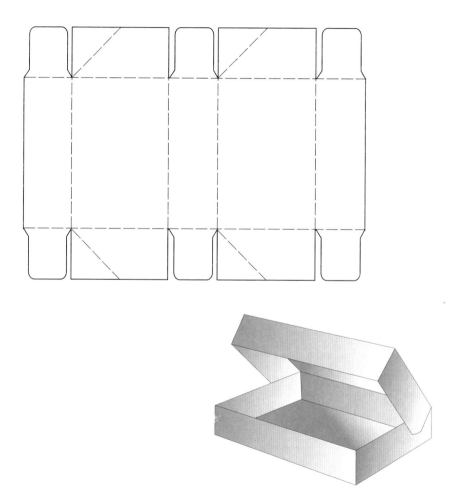

Heavy duty carton with carry handle

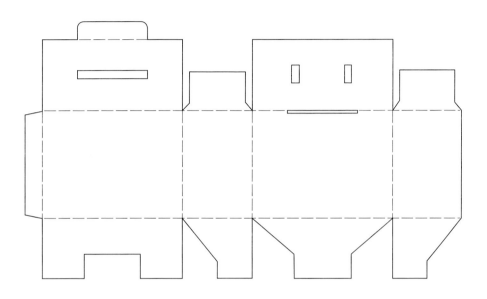

Tapered side carton with double tuck-in flaps

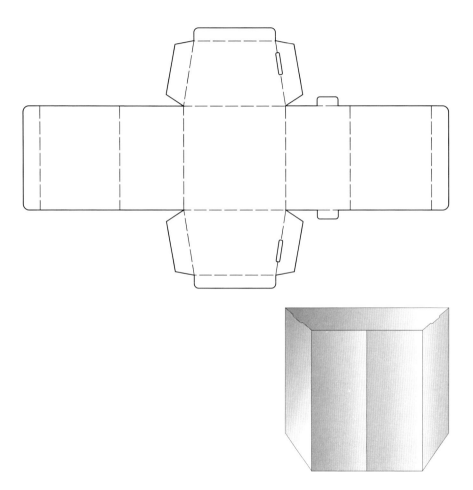

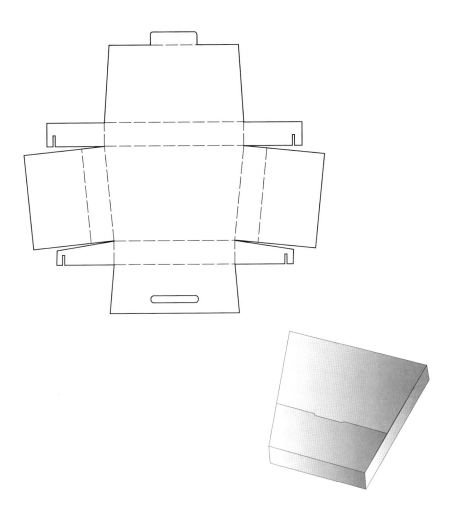

Sealed type, tear open package

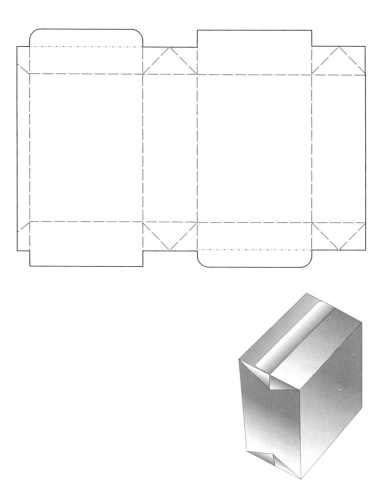

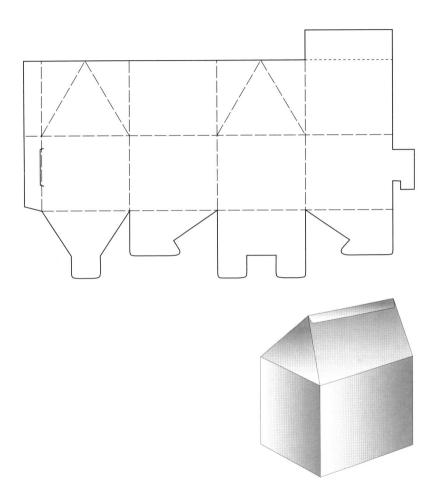

Heavy duty tray & sleeve drawer type carton

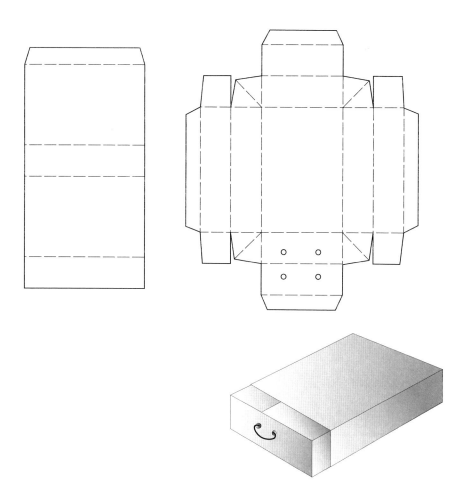

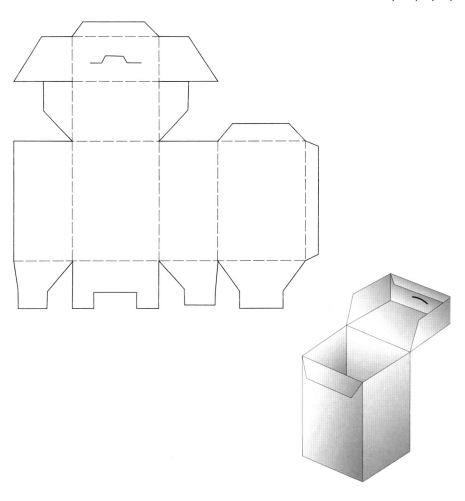

Tapered bottom with hinged lid

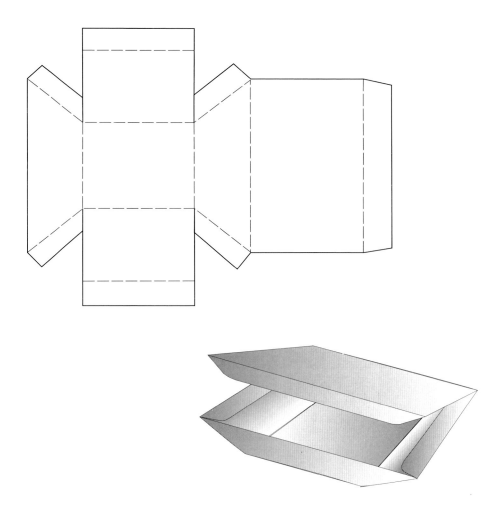

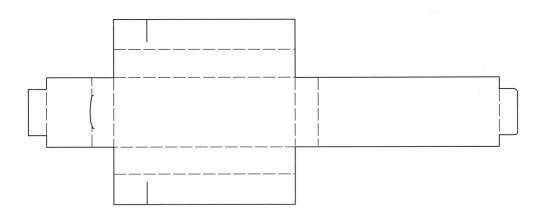

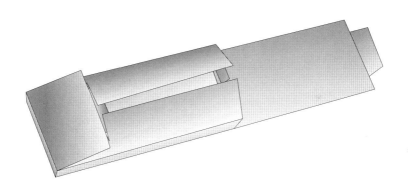

Folder type carton with double decker tray

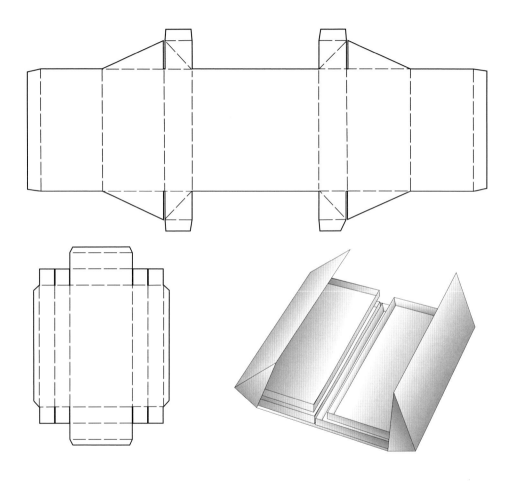

Tray with hinged lid and front panel tuck-in lock

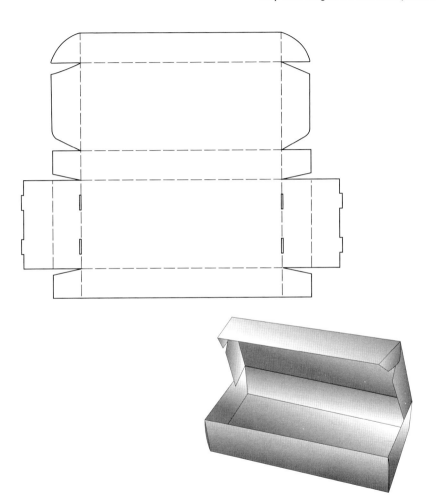

Wrap around for gift package

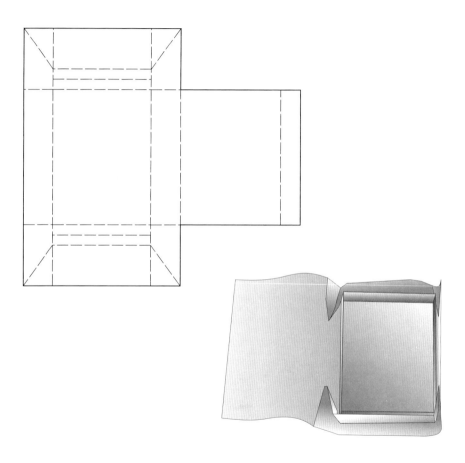

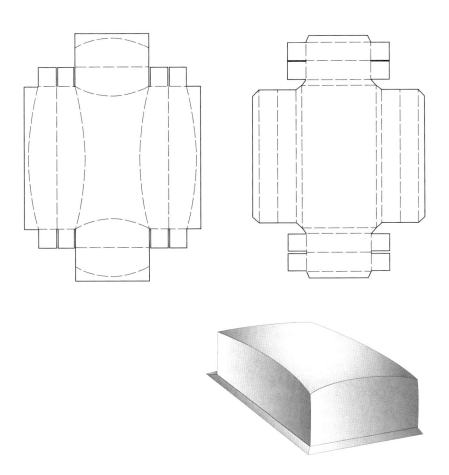

Gift package

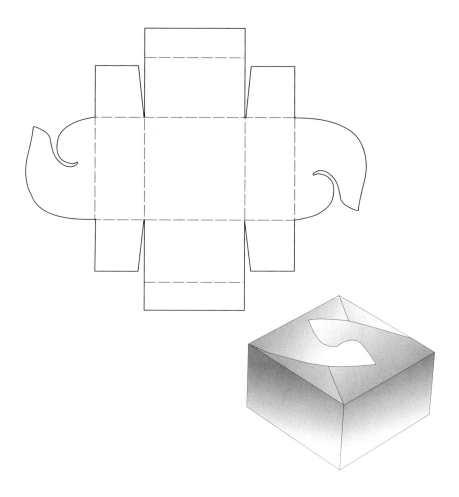

Gift package

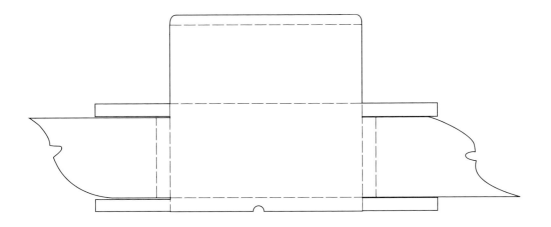

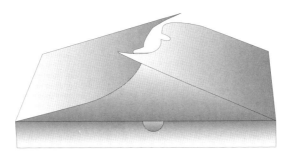

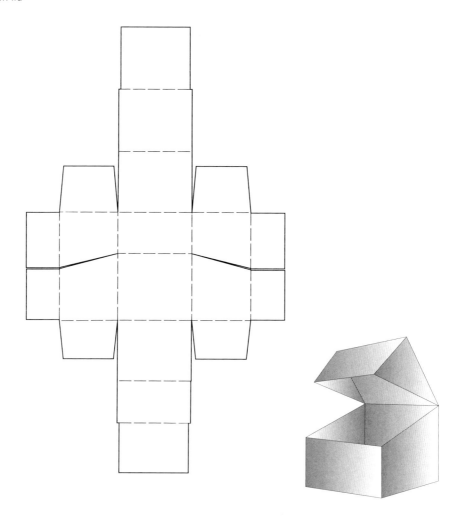

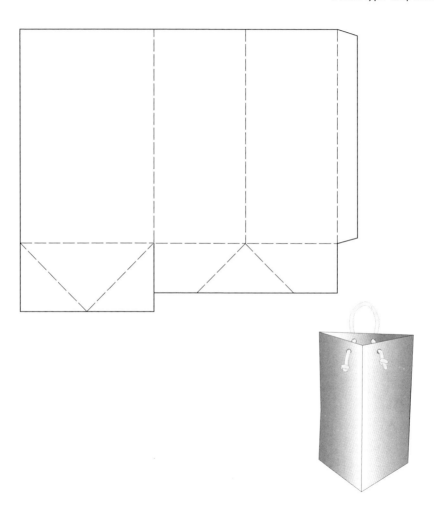

Tab lock tray

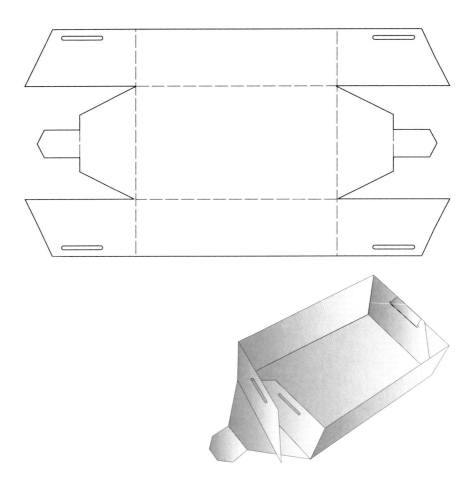

Gusseted side lock tray, hinged lid with dust flap and top tab lock

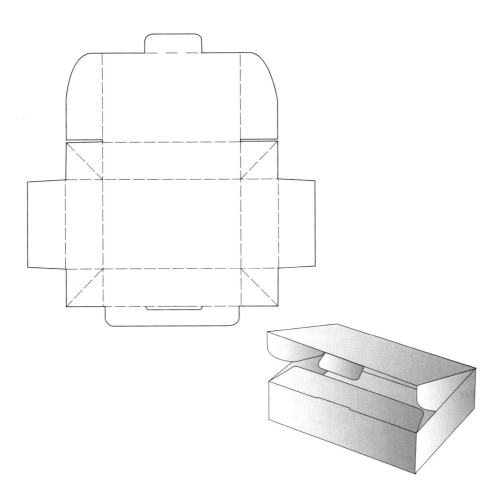

Gusseted side lock tray, hinged lid with dust flap and bottom tab lock

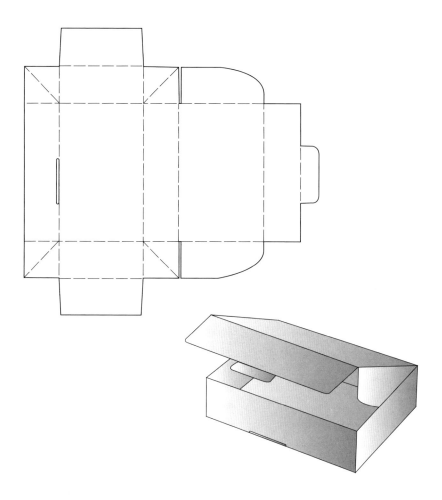

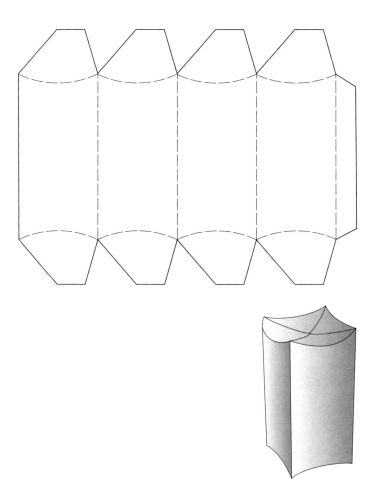

Diamond shape package

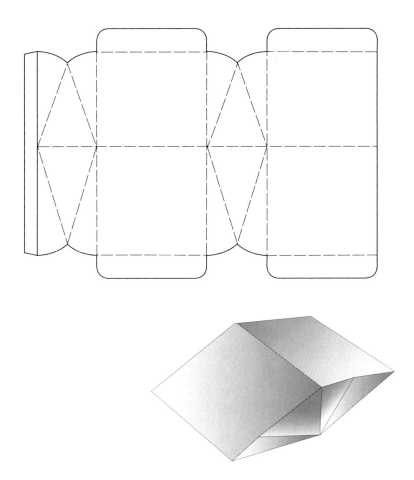

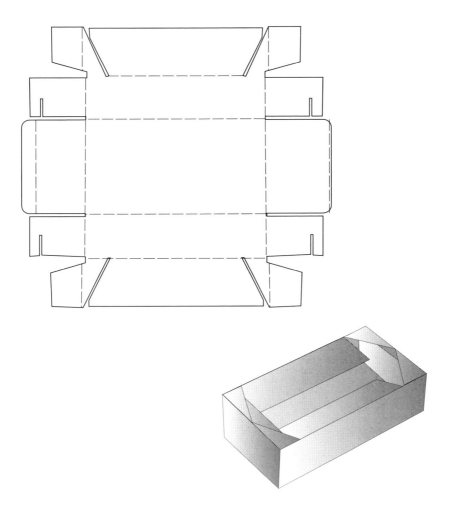

Transperant pvc package

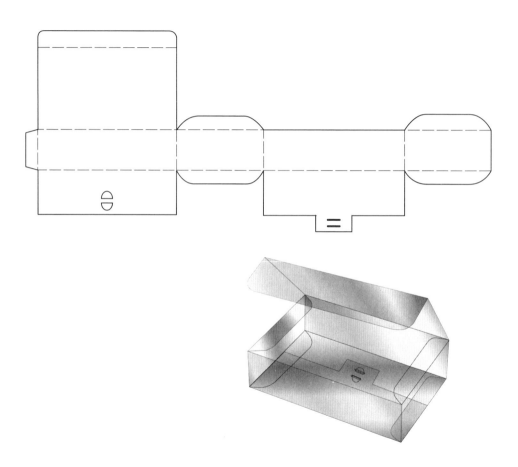

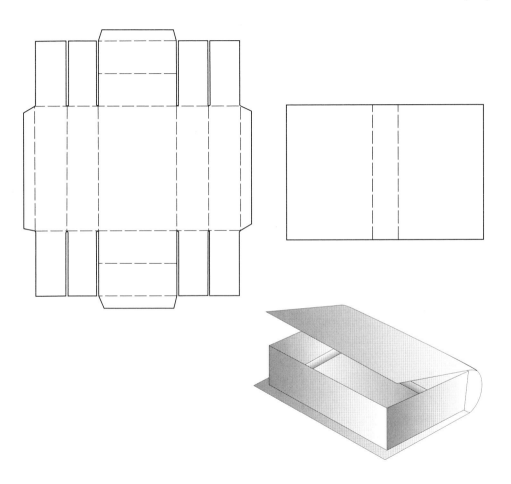

Gusseted side tray with double side wall lid

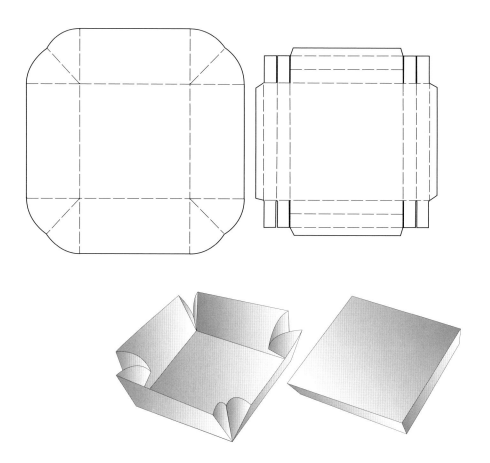

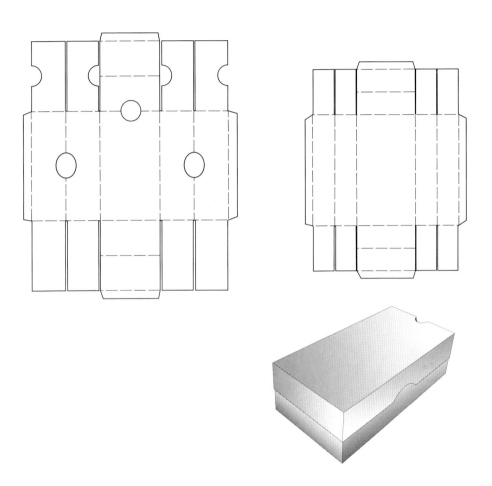

Twin hinged box with windows

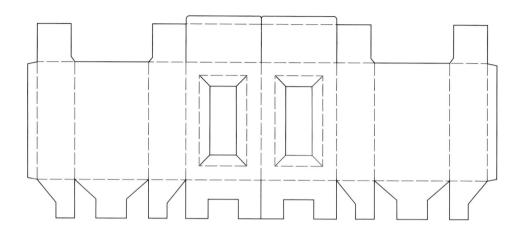

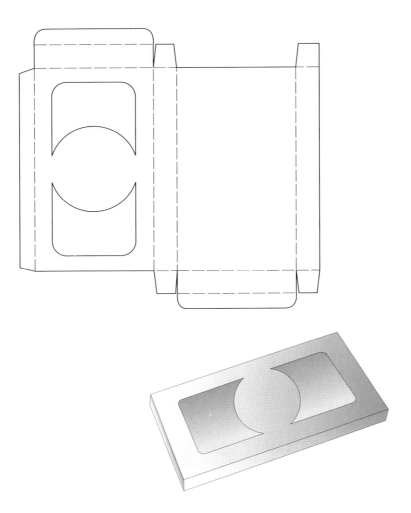

Transparent carton

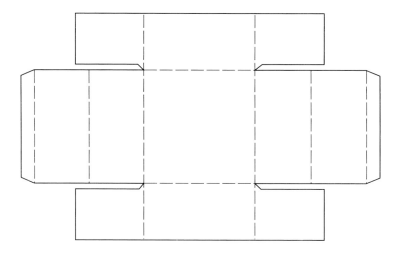

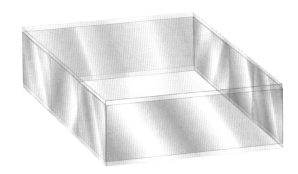

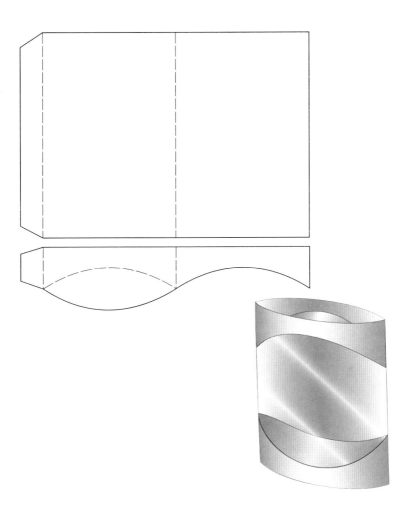

Carton with telescopic lid and window

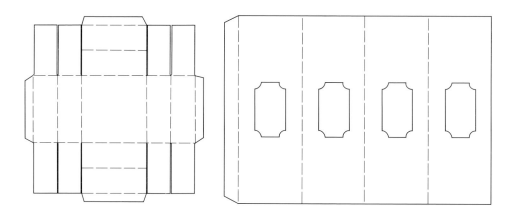

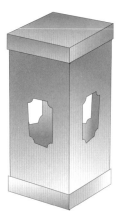

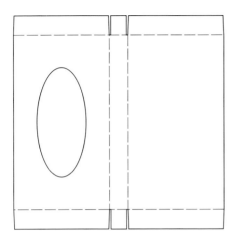
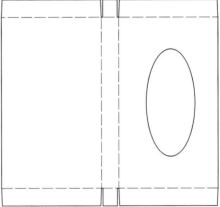
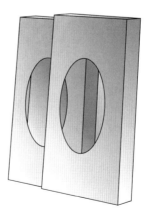

Reverse tuck carton with window display

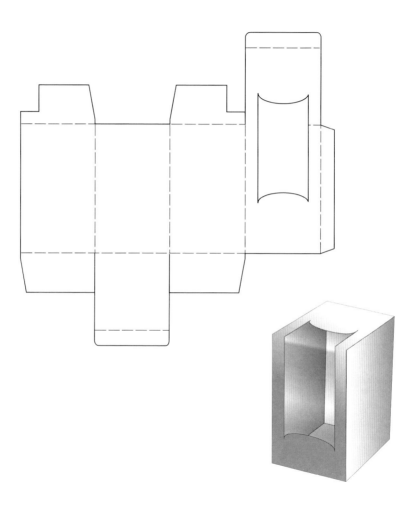

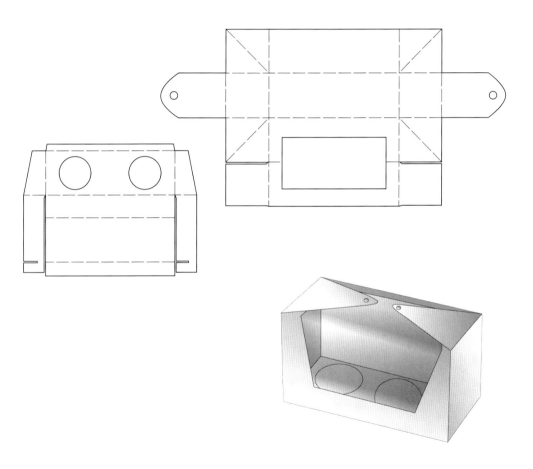

Stackable type Bottom and Lid Carton

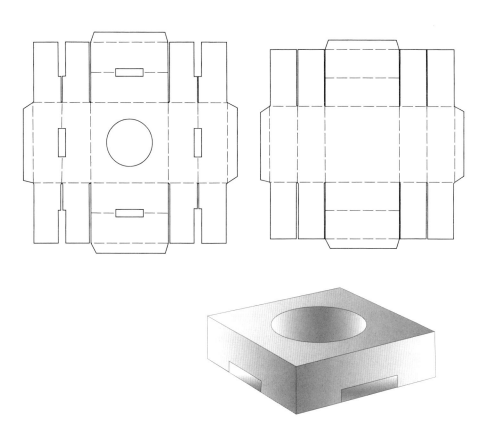

Auto assemble carton with window

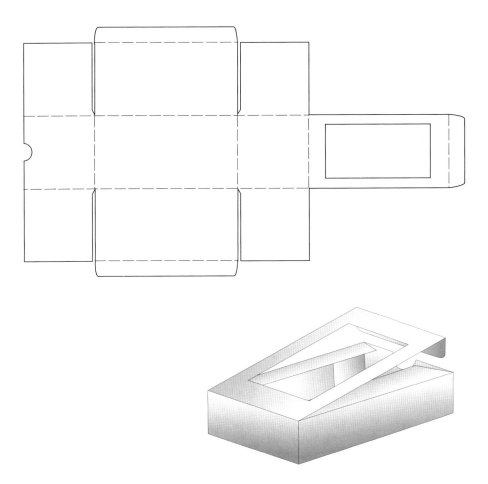

Two sided window carton with hanging panel

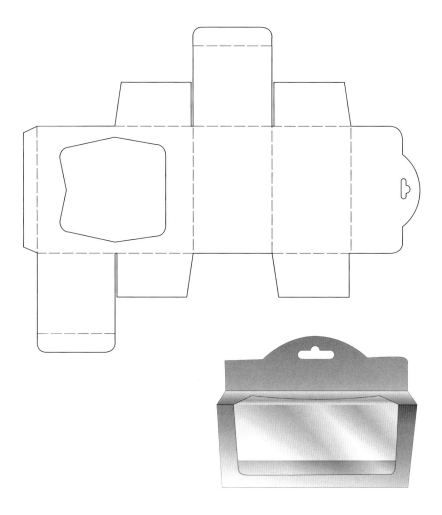

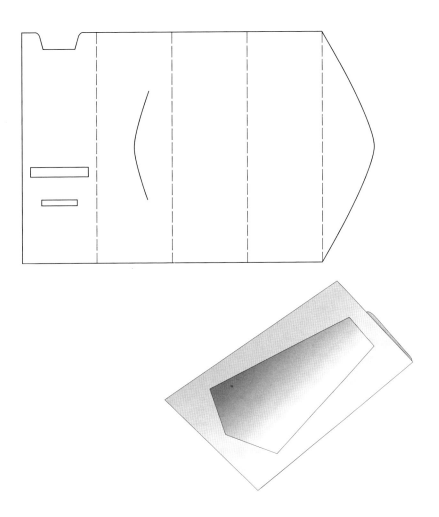

Double wall tray/lid with window

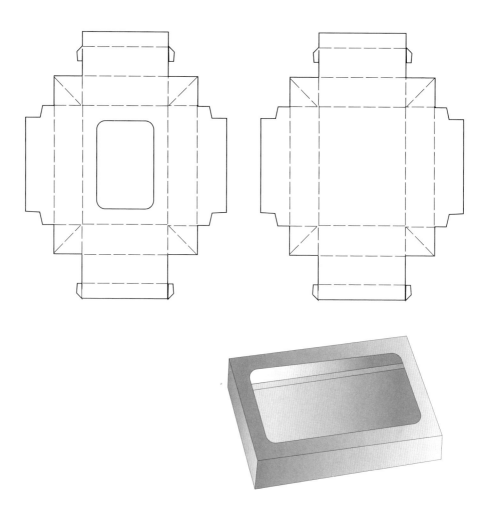

Auto lock bottom window carton with tapered side

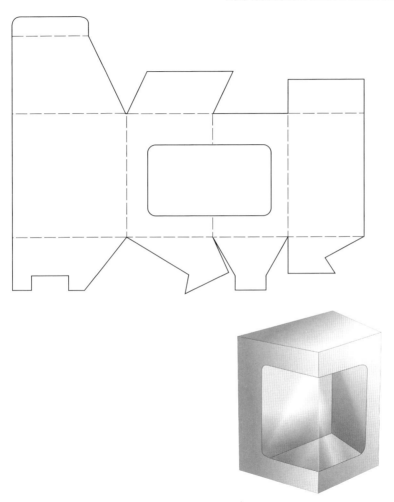

Haxagonal carton with window display

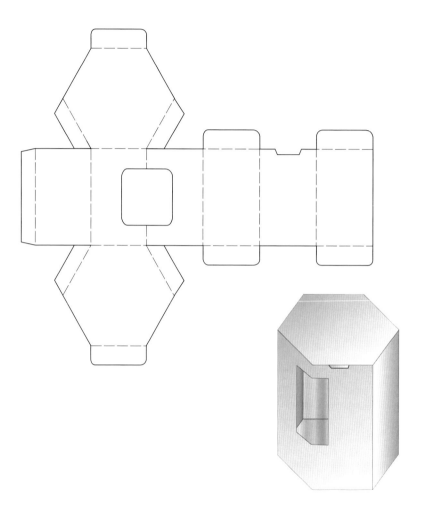

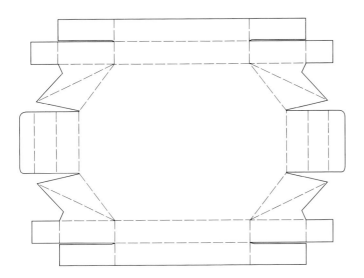

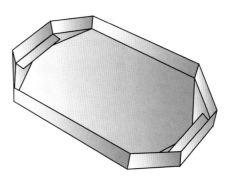

Single piece triple decker hanging carton

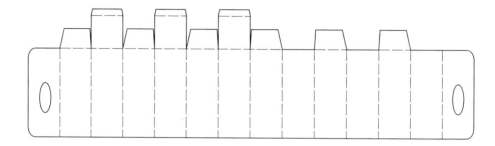

Four side dome top with hook locks tuck-in flaps

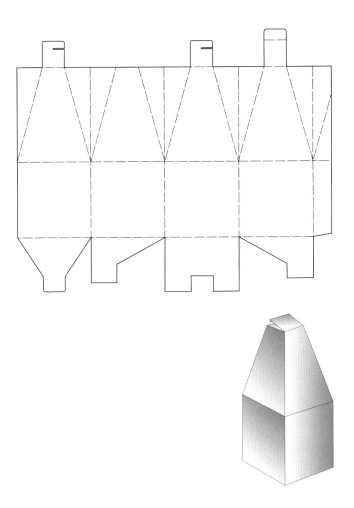

Sleeve & double wall slinding traywith tapered corner

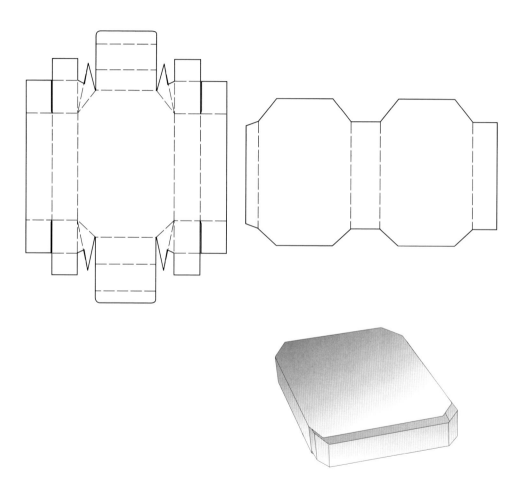

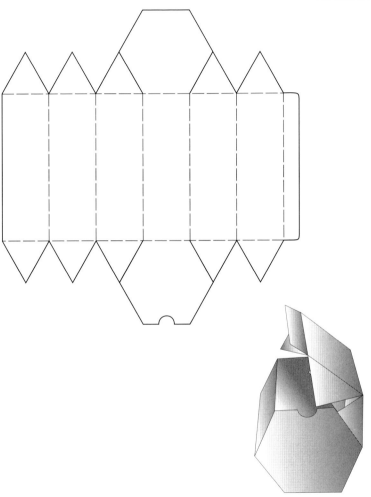

Wide mouth opening Carton

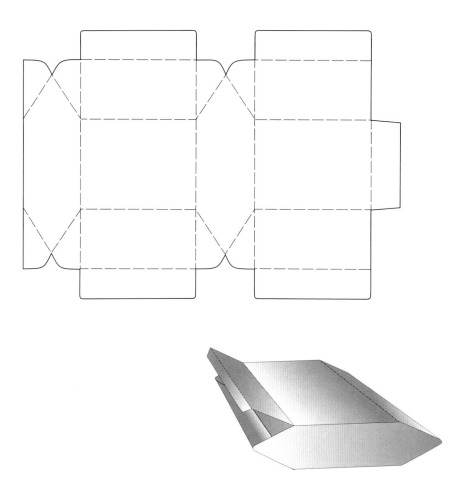

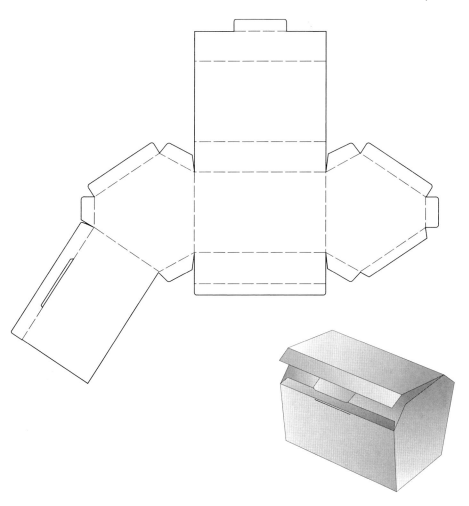

Tapered walls tray with double wall lid

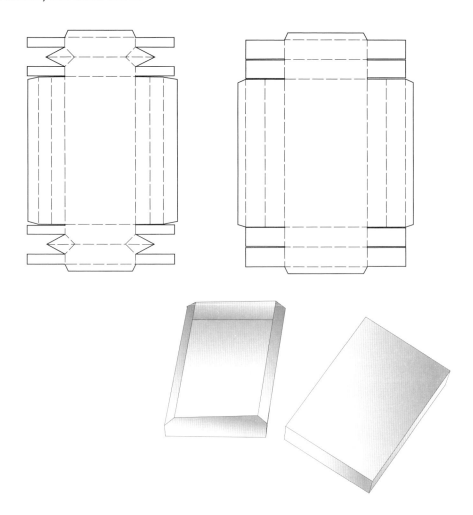

Tapered sides half rounded top flap

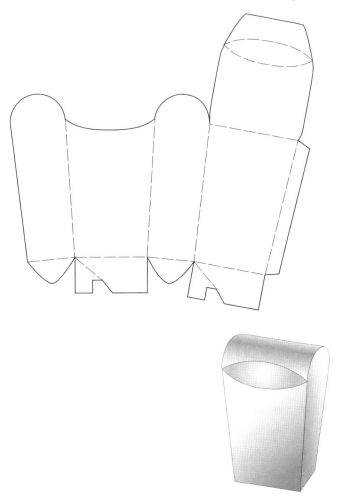

Self locking six sides carton

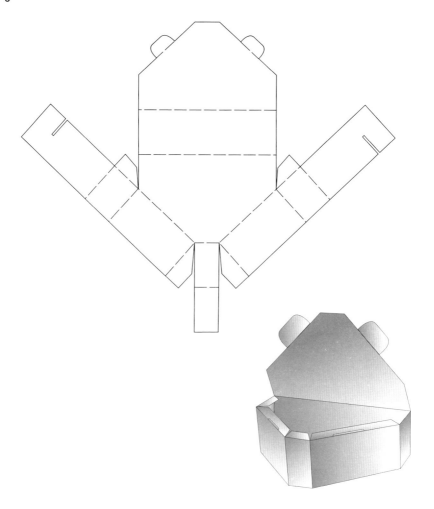

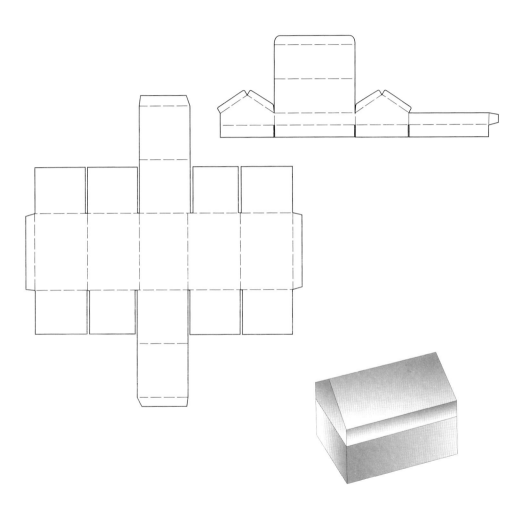

Double wall tray with house type lid

Single piece self locking house shaped carton

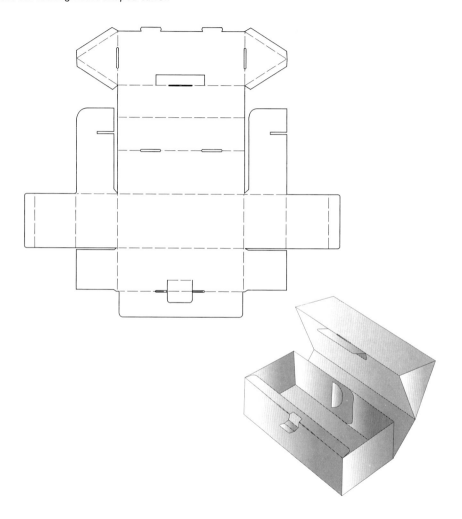

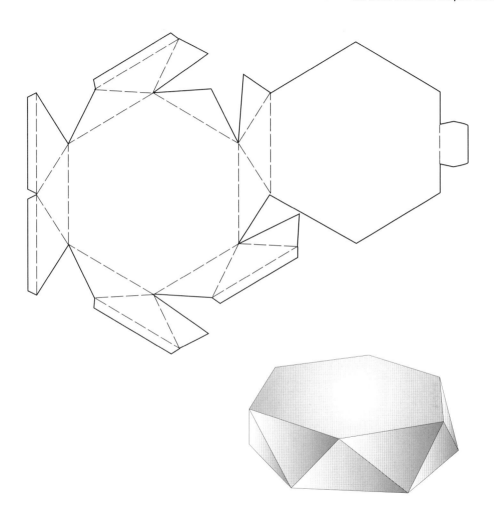

Twelve side rounded wall tray/lid

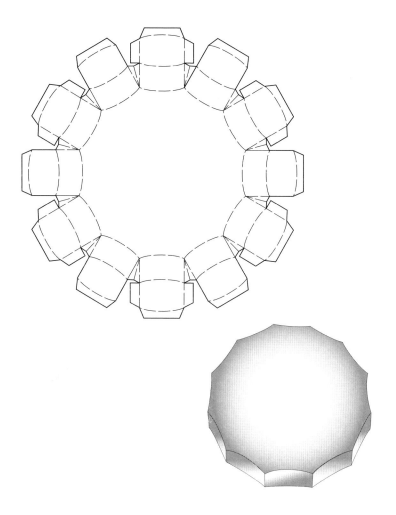

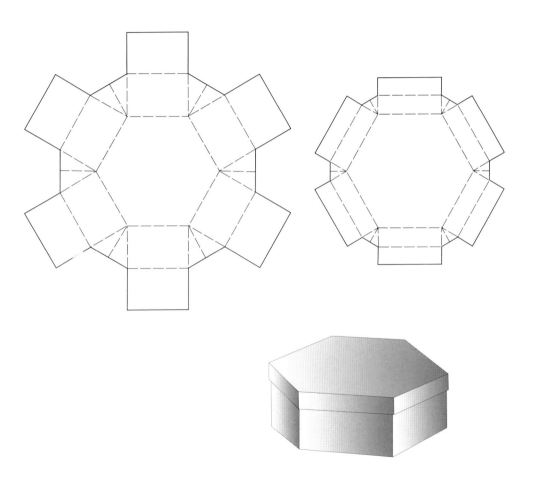

Hexagonal gift carton

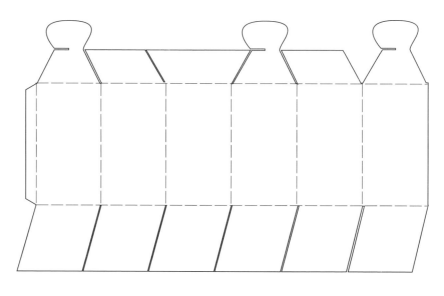

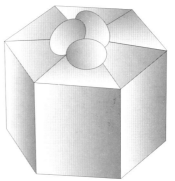

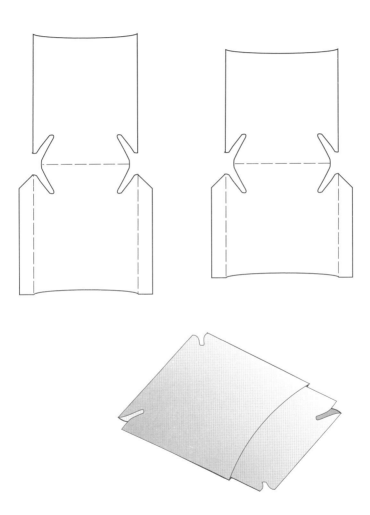

Strait tuck carton with curved sides

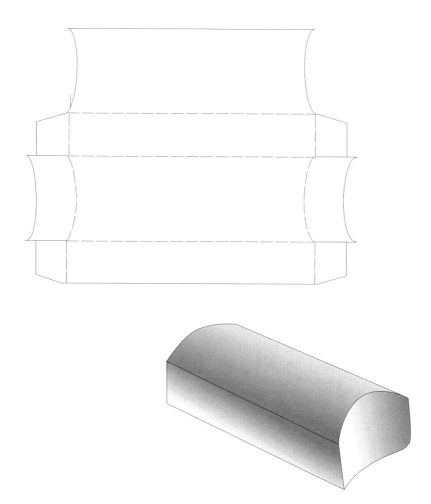

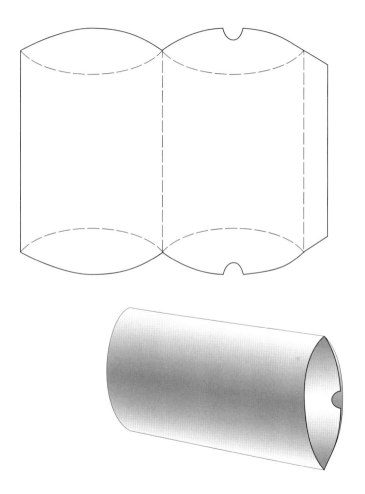

One side open pillow pack

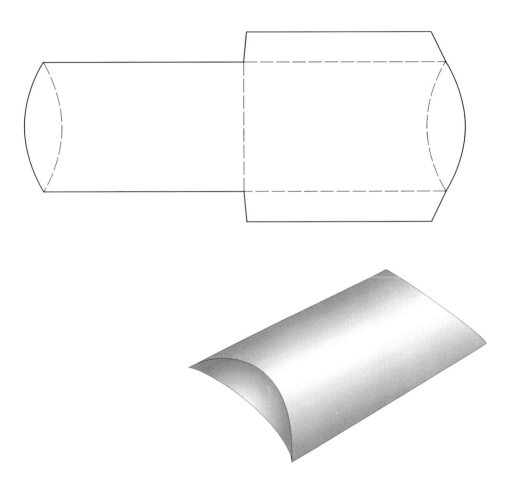

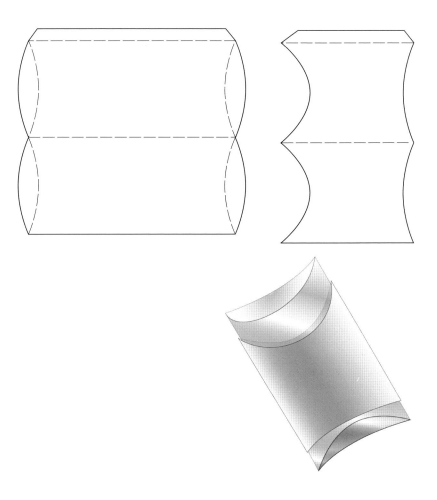

Transparent pillow pack with sleeve

Pillow pack with tuck in flap

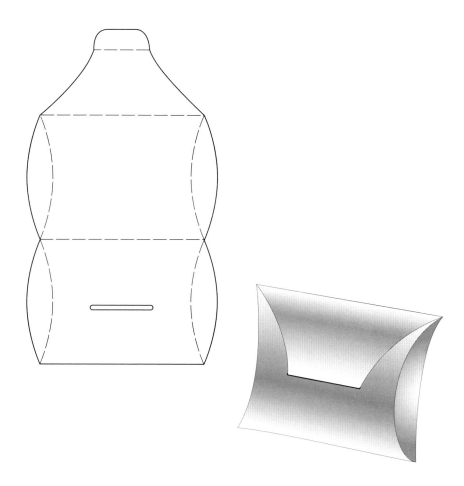

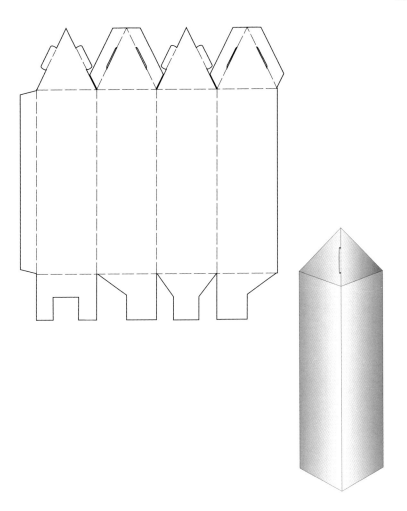

Gift pack

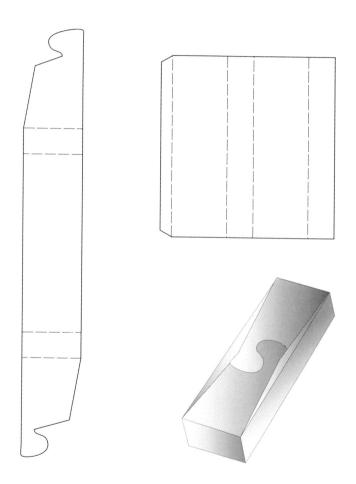

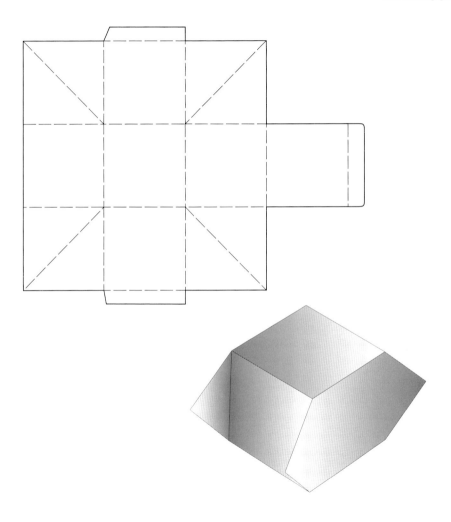

Book type Window Carton

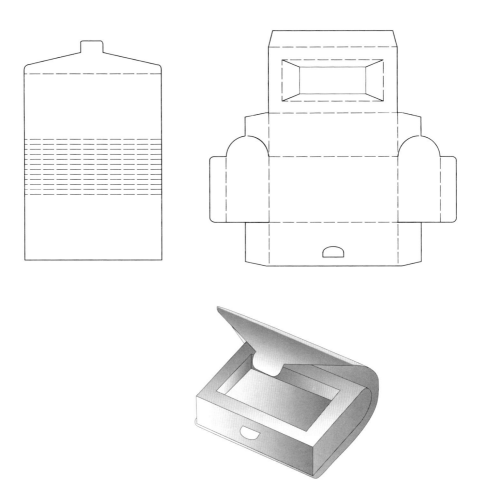

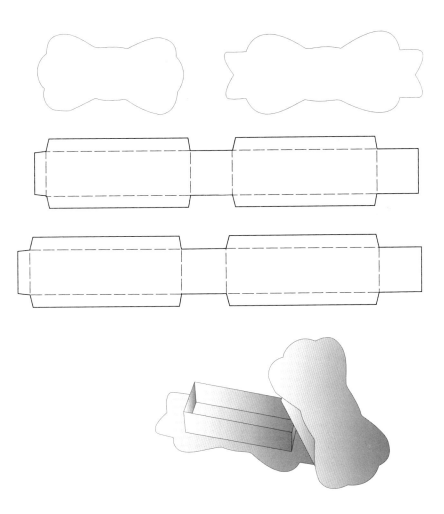

Self & inter locking gift pack

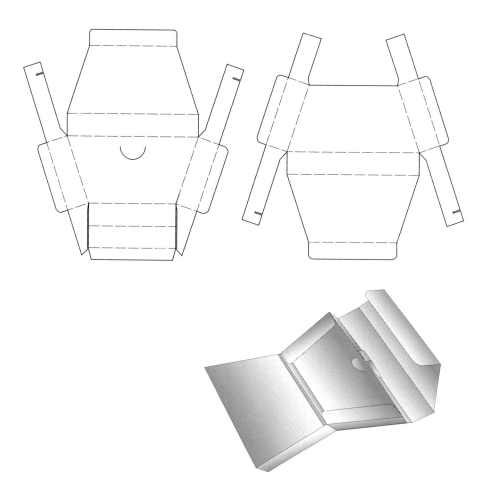

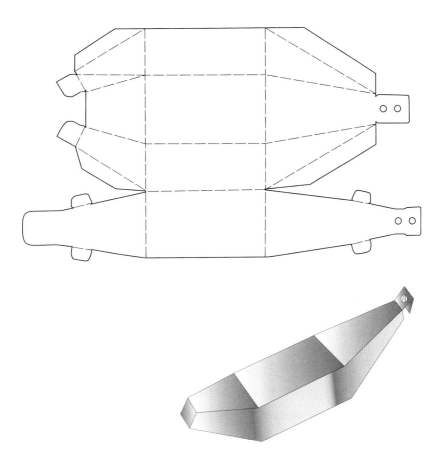

Bag type tapered sides carton

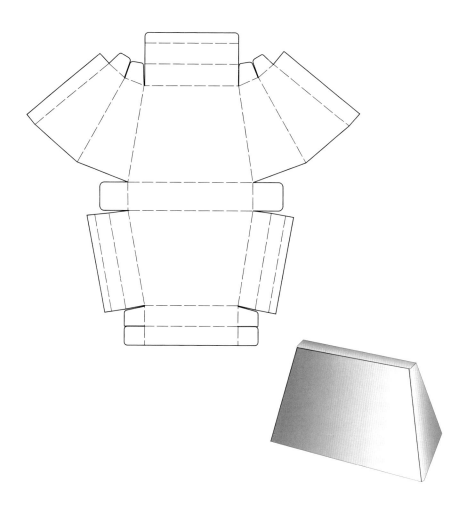

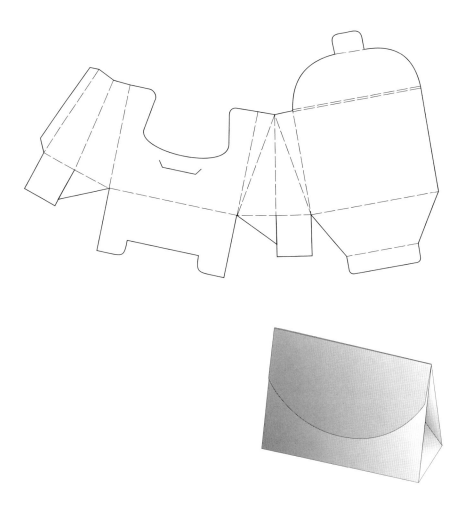

Heart shaped set up carton

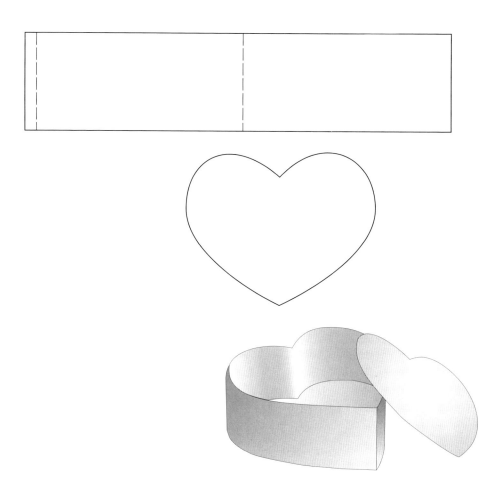

One side open triangular insert with sleeve

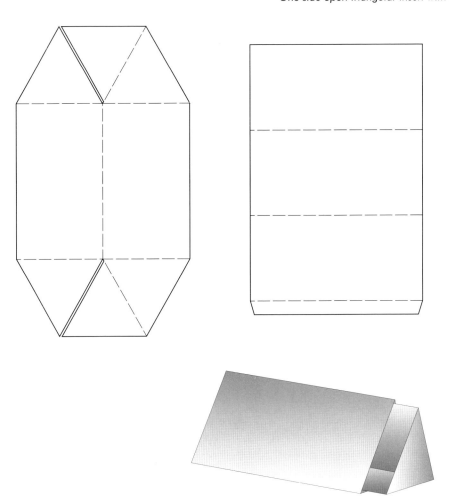

Round corner gift pack

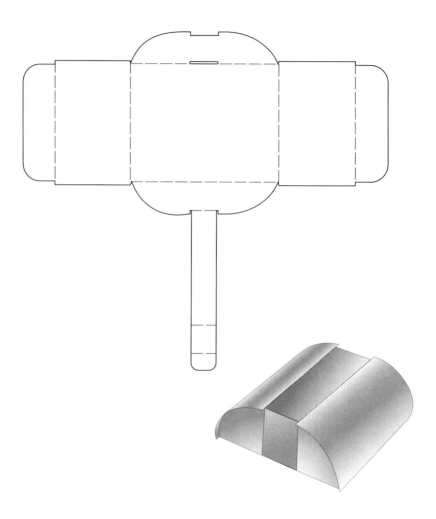

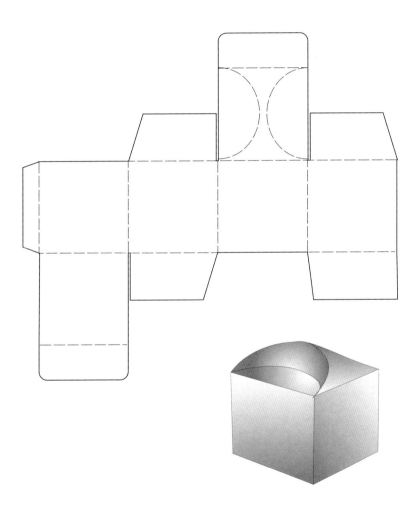

Triangular top/bottom curved crease carton

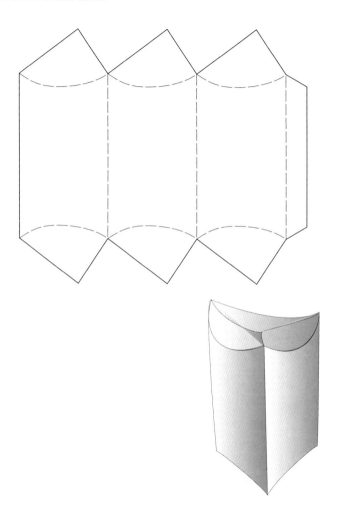

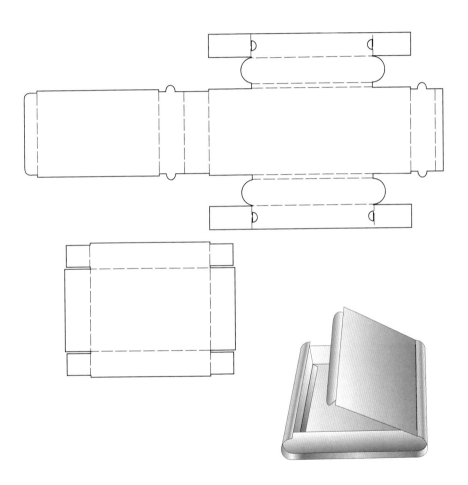

Rounded lid and bottom Carton with flip open lid

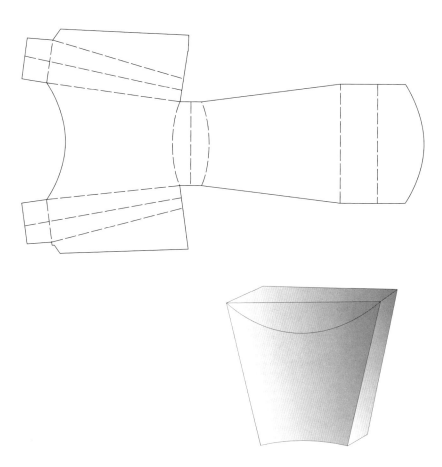

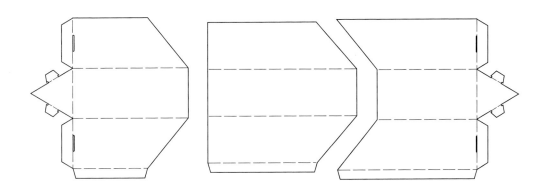

X'mas tree shaped top/bottom carton

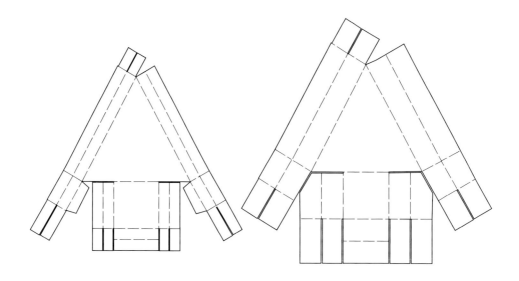

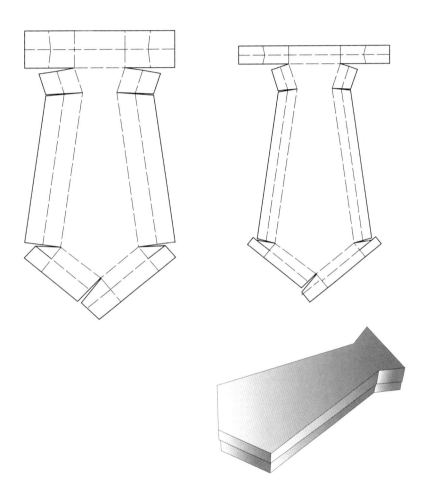

Self locking one piece tray/lid with window

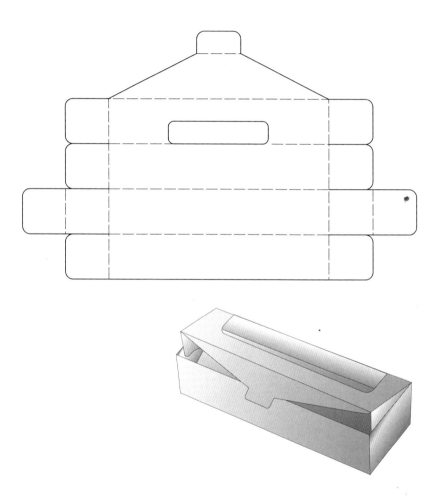

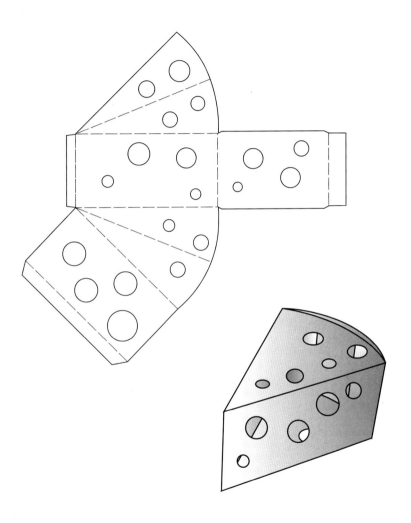

Seven panel bag type carton with partition & handle

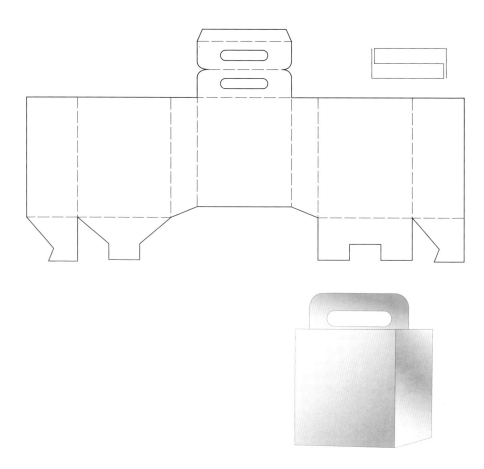

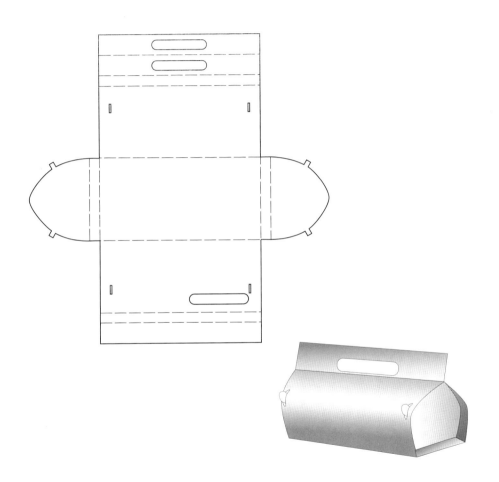

Vertical carton with handles built in ear locks

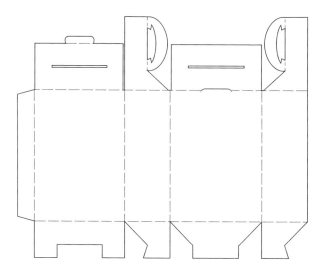

Hexagonal carton variation with handle

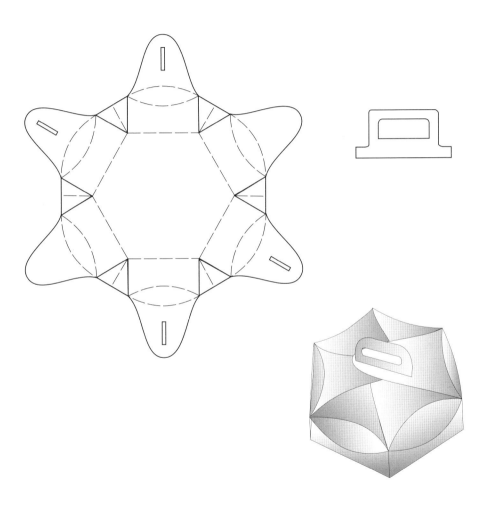

Variation in carton with handle

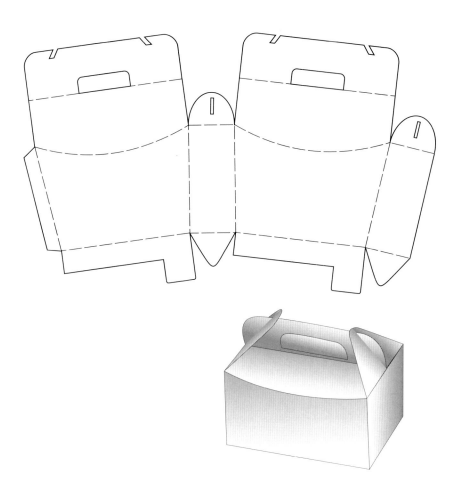

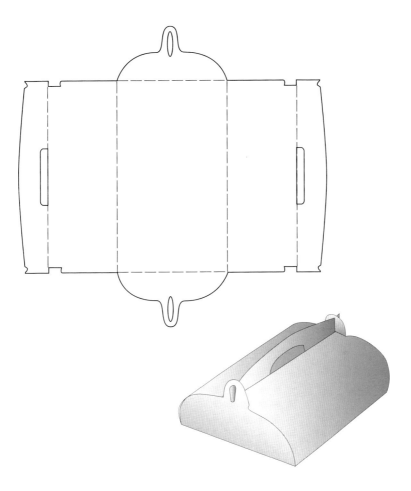

Hexagonal carton with handle

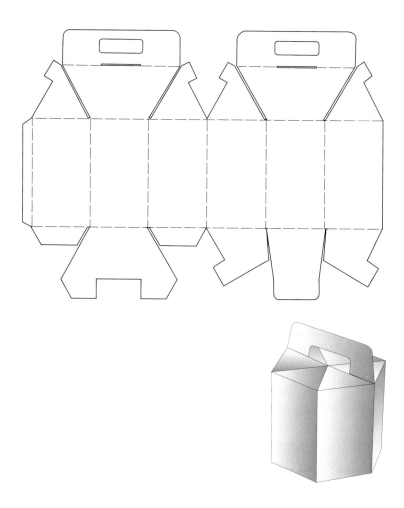

Diamond shaped carton with handle & side lockings

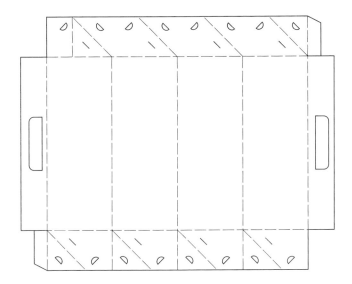

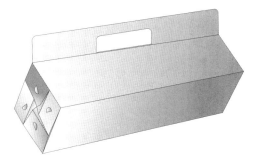

Tapered top carton with handle

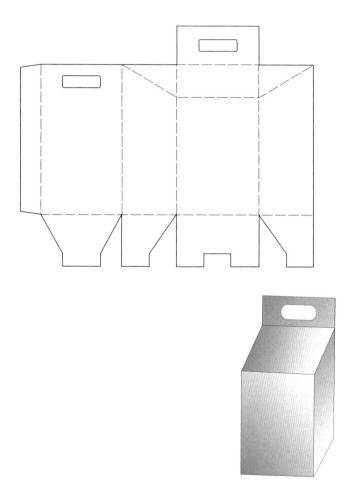

Tapered tray carton with handle & side lockings

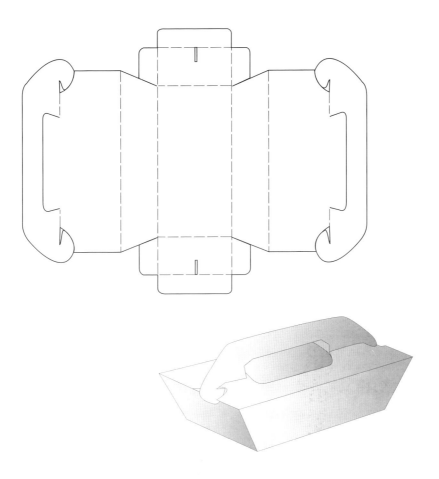

Briefcase type carton

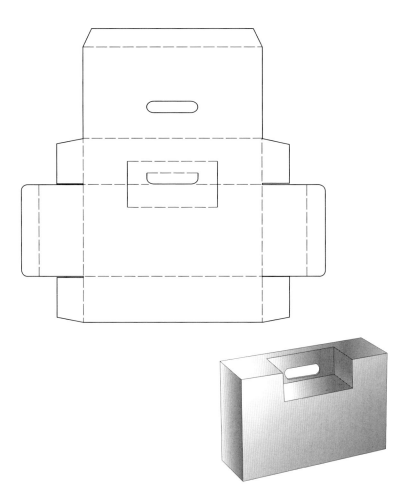

Carrier type carton

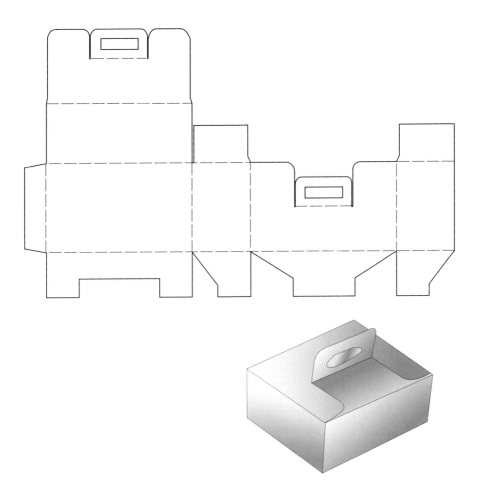

Half-cut Hexagonal Carry on Carton

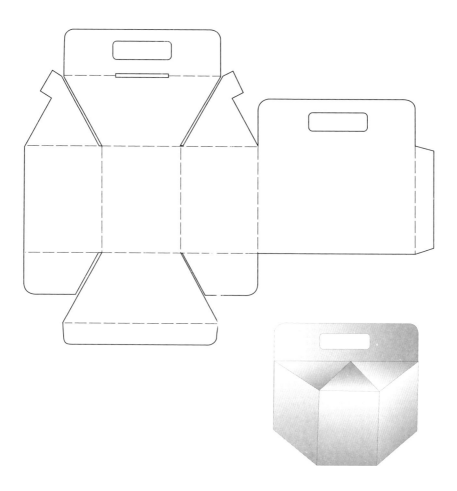

Tapered top vertical carton with handle

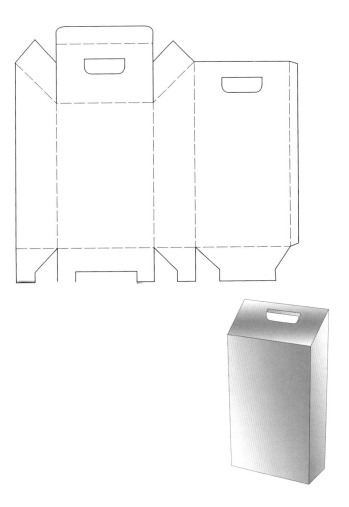

Hanging type Straight Tuck Carton

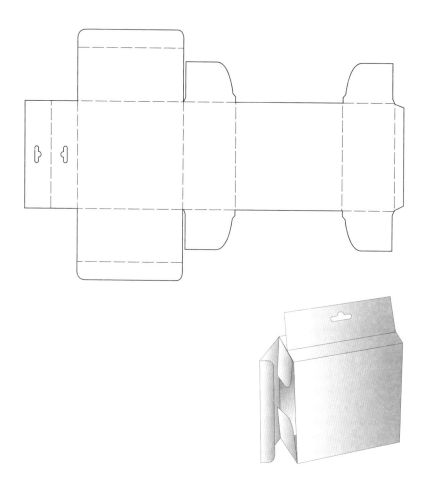

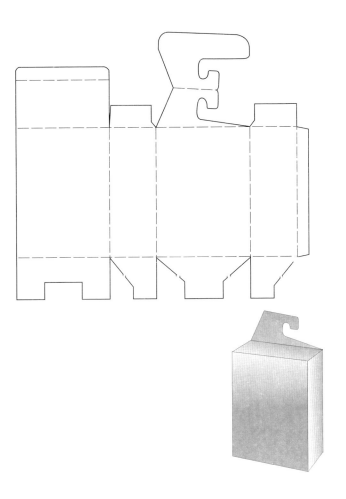

Hut shaped carton with handle

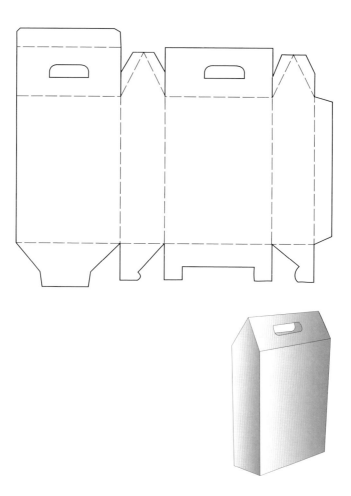

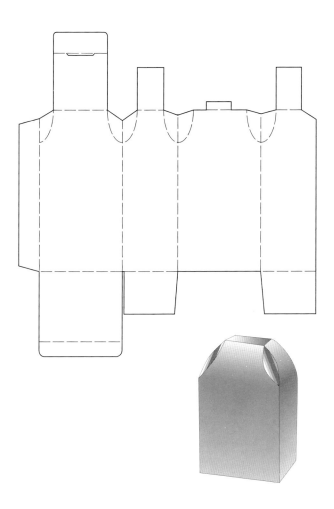

Cheese/Butter self assembly carton

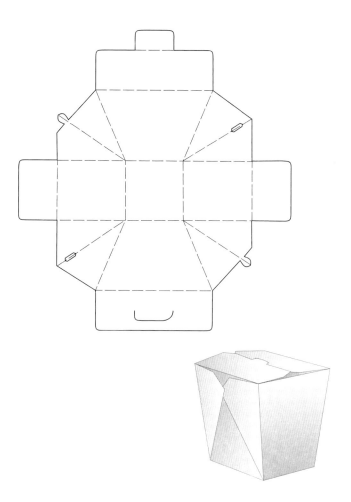

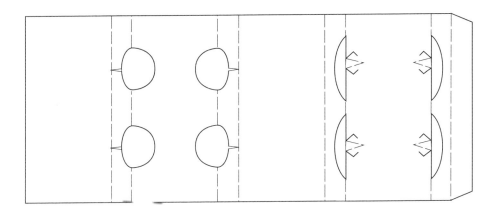

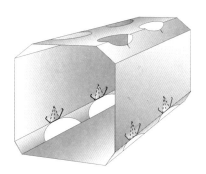

Six Bottle Carry-type Pack

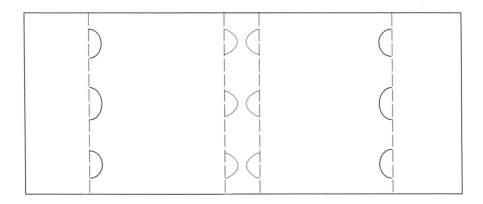

DISPLAY CARTONS

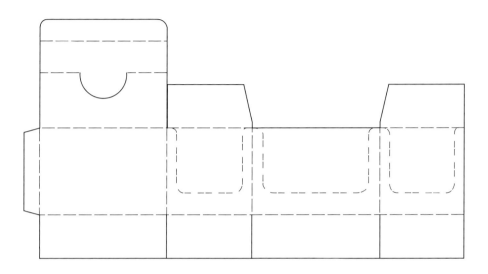

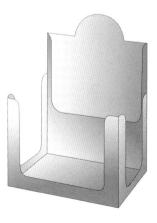

Display Cartons 133

Double wall display with windows

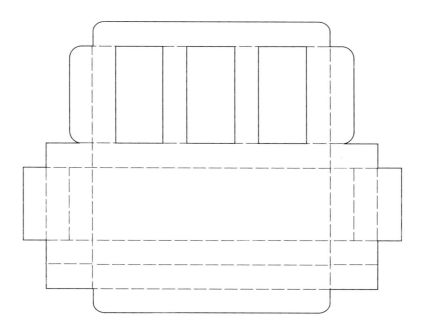

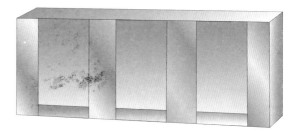

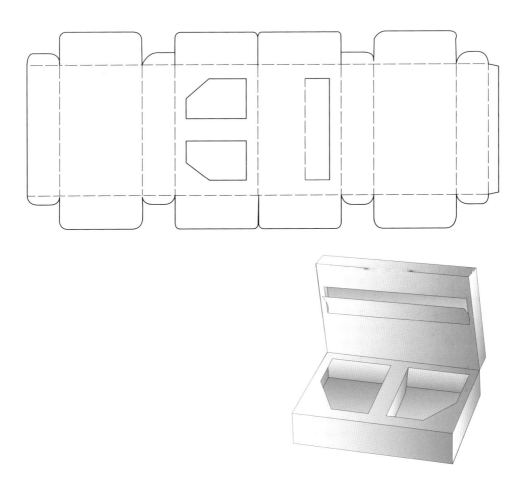

Double wall carton with inner display platform

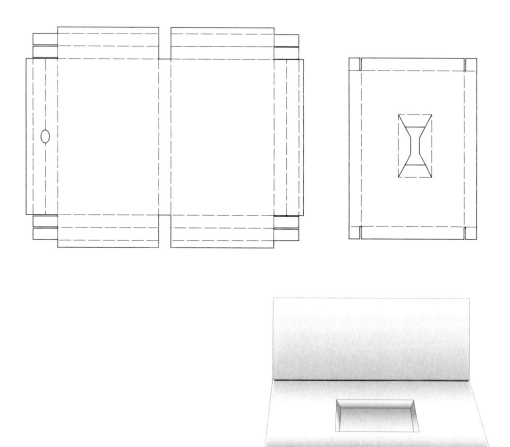

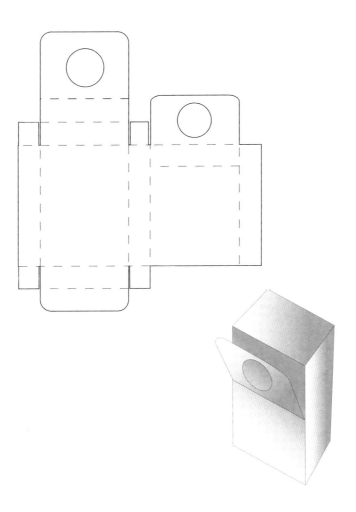

Straight tuck carton with fifth back drop panel

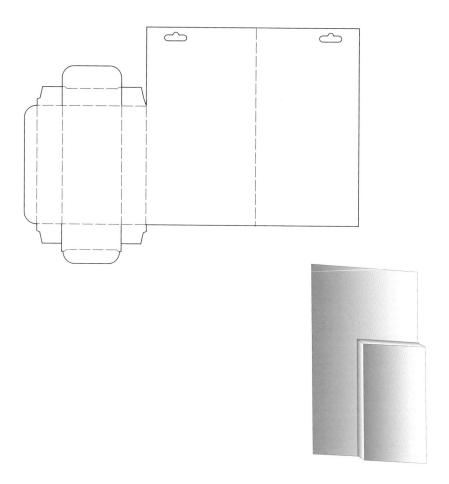

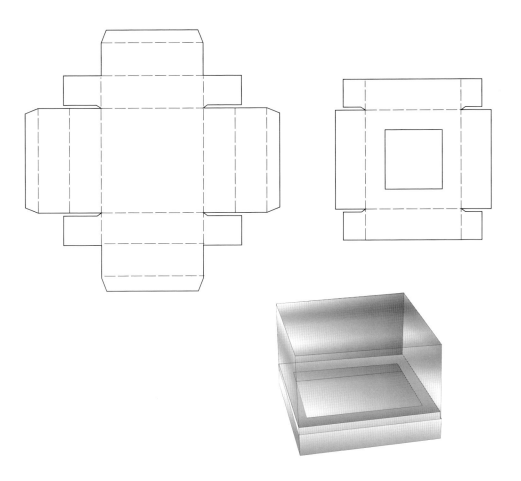

Double wall tray/lid with platform

Double wall tray & liner with partition window & handle

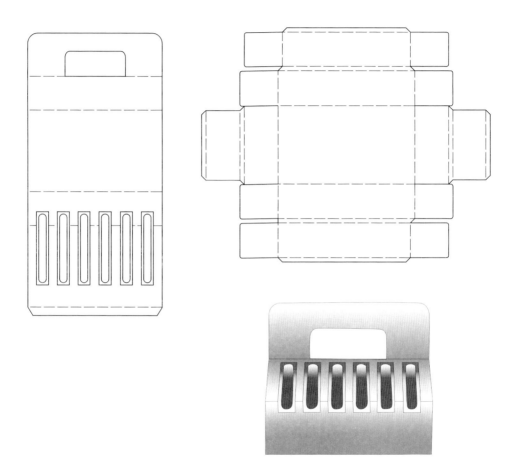

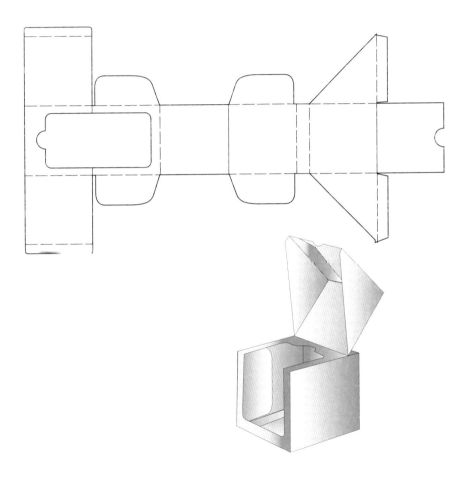

Self locking one piece tray/lid with separate partitions

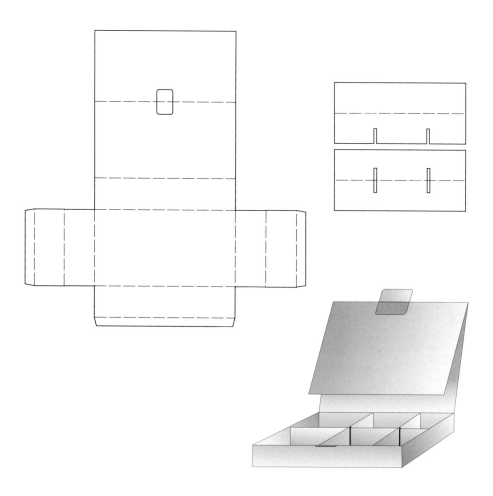

Self locking one piece triangle shape display

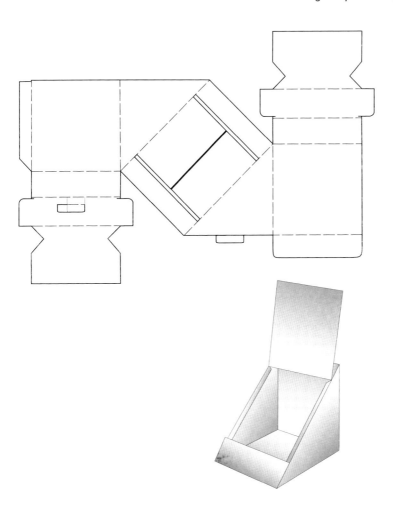

Sefl asse3mble tpye Display Carton

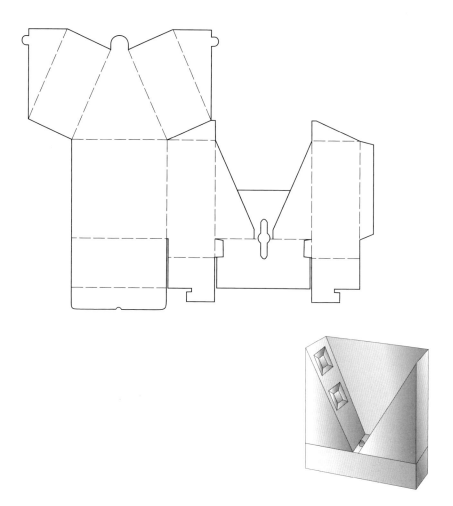

Self locking one piece tray/lid with built in partitions

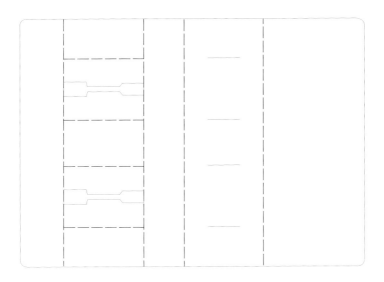

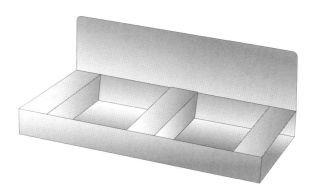

Press lock Carton with tear open display top flep

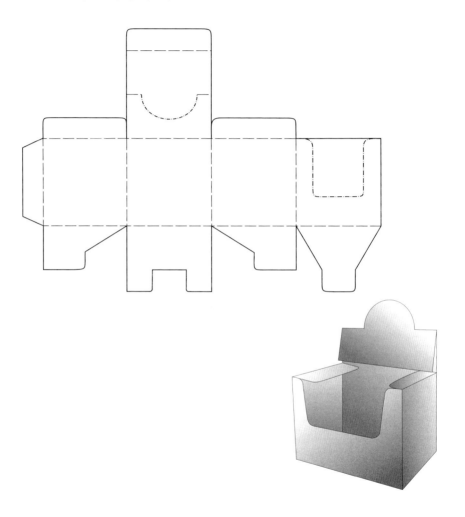

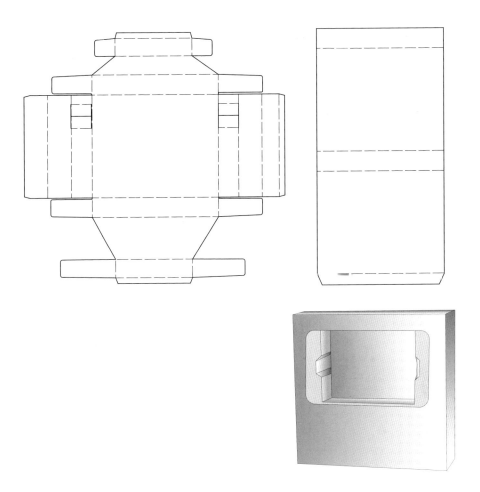

Reverse tuck carton with hinged lid & self cavity tray

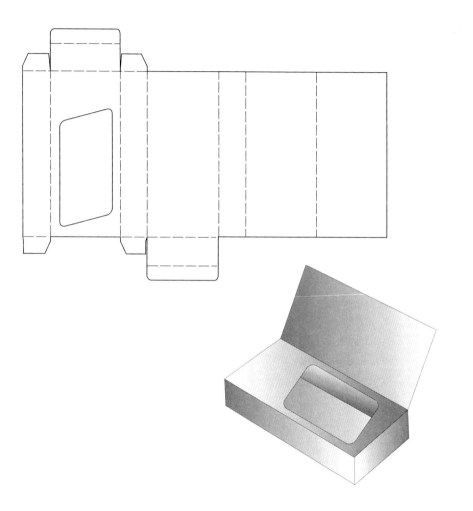

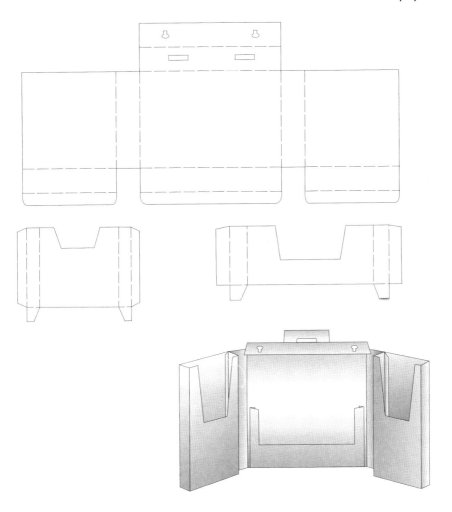

Self locking single piece folder type display

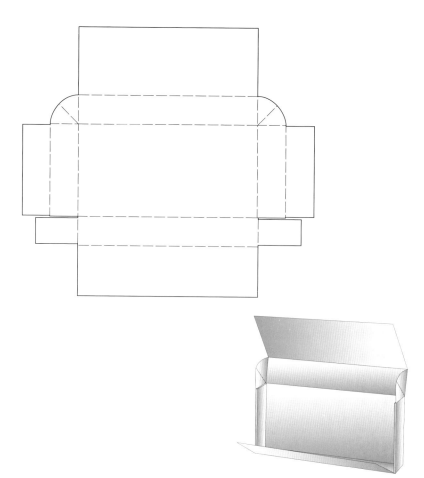

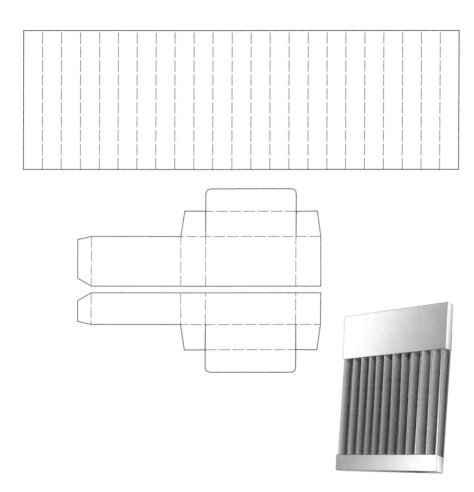

Tear Open Top Display Carton

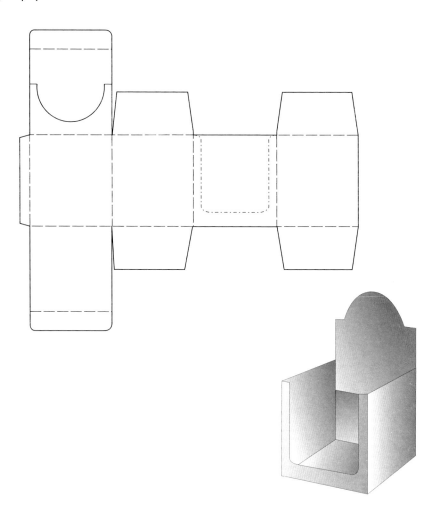

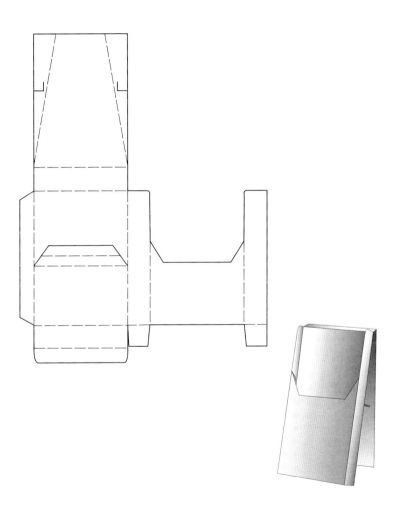

Straight tuck carton converted to tray type display

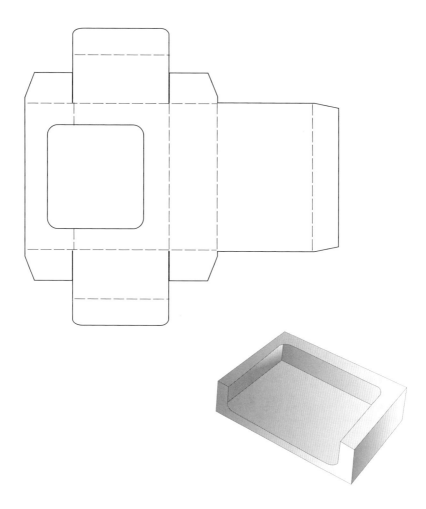

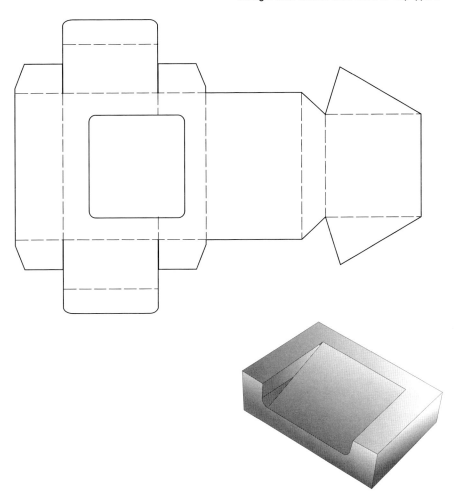

Straight tuck carton converted to tray type slant display

Faceted top with window display

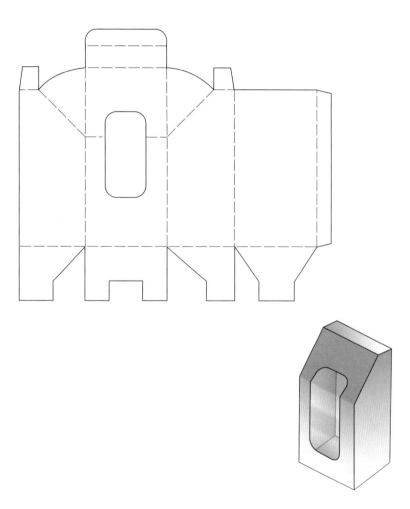

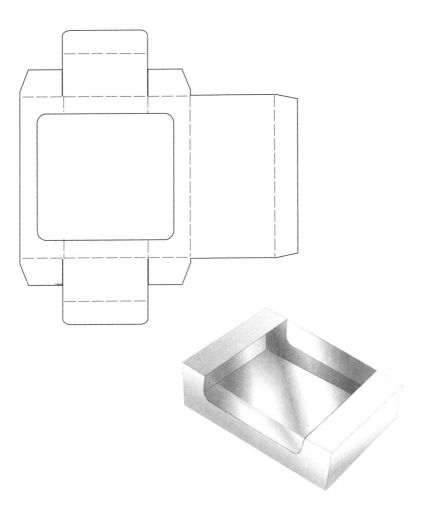

Hinged top with built in partition

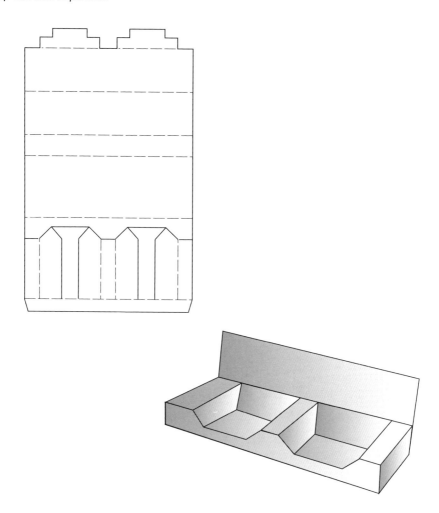

DISPENSERS

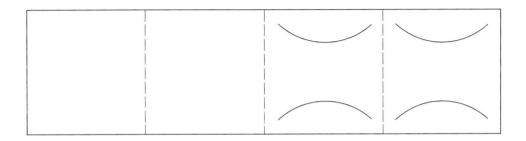

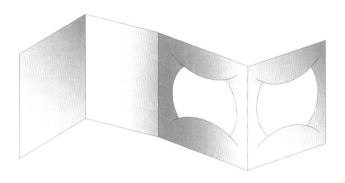

One piece self locking carrier type dispenser with sleeve

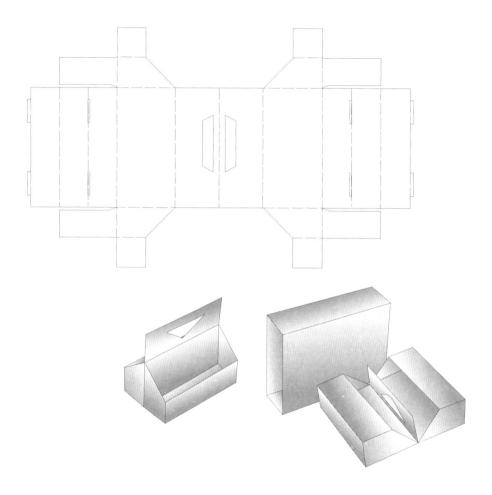

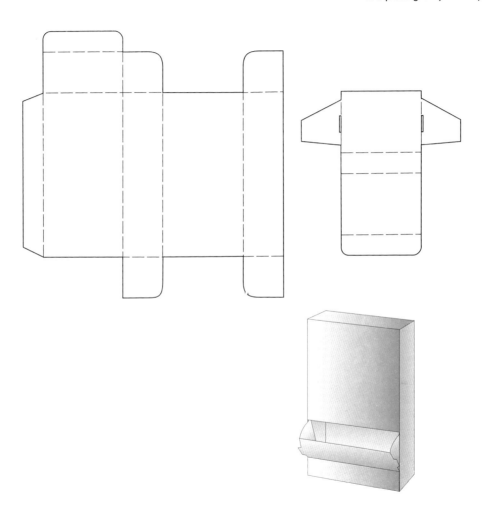

Two piece gravity-fed dispenser

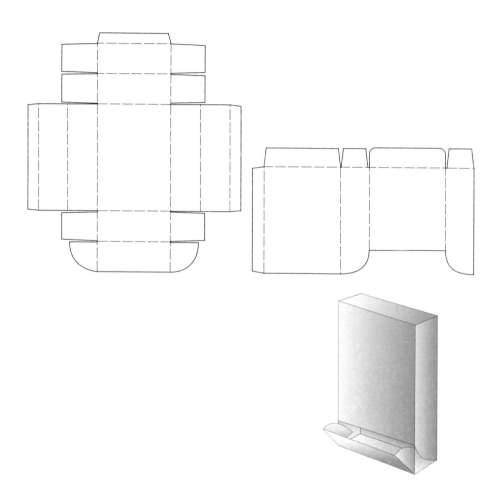

Single piece self locking dispenser

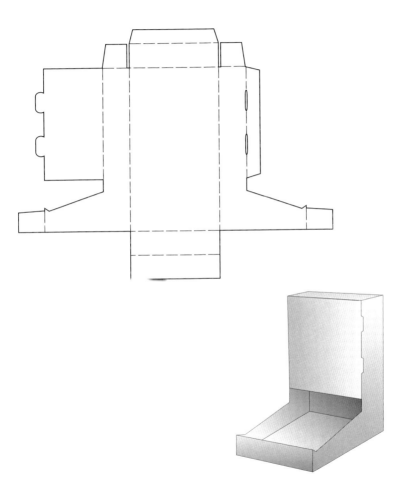

Two hanging self locking dispenser with back supporter

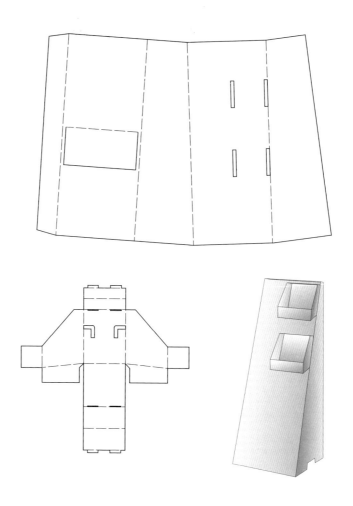

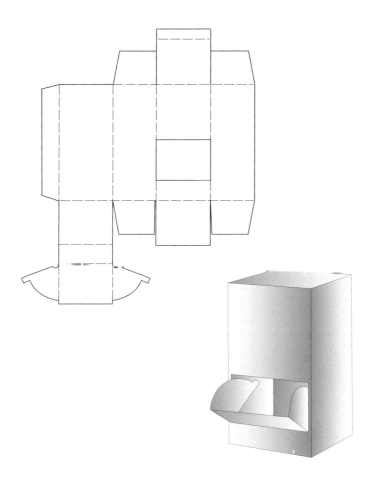

Two piece gravity-fed dispenser with built in partition

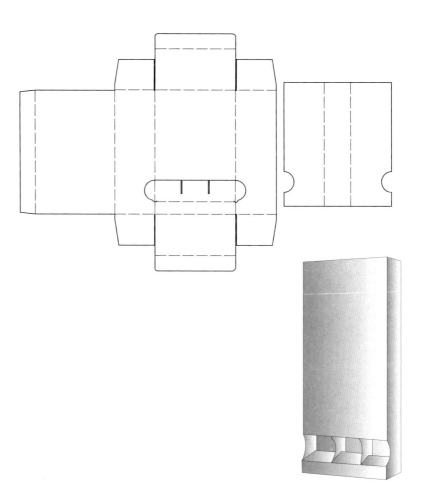

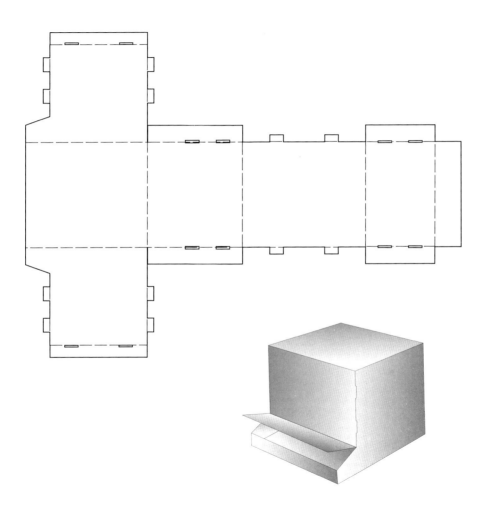

Single piece gravity-fed dispenser variation

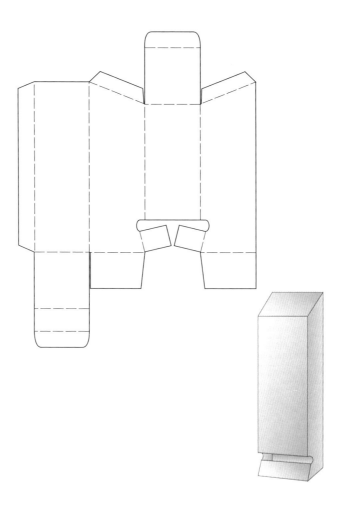

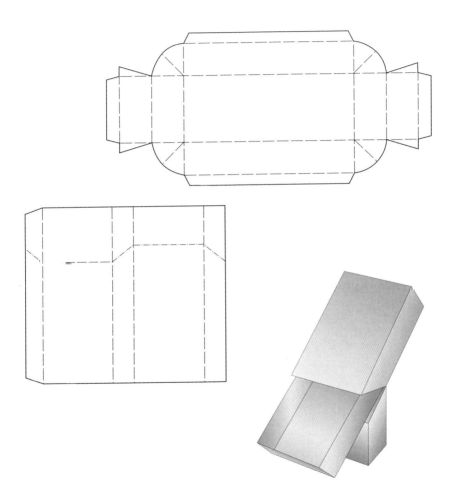

Single piece tapered dispenser

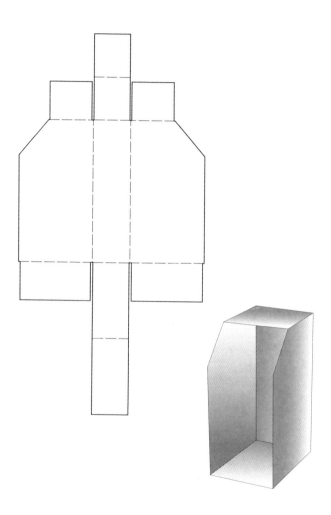

DISPLAYS & POP'S

Two piece tray/lid dispenser where, lid used as holder

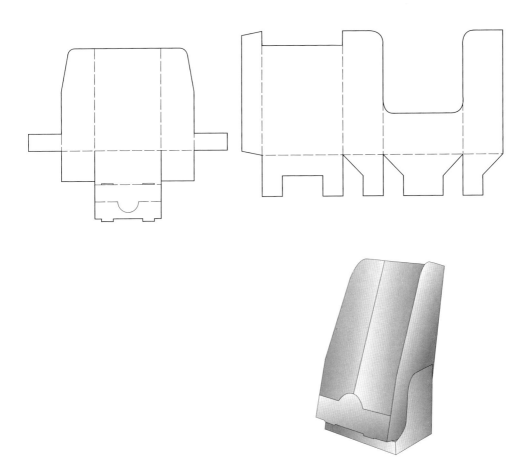

Six panels dispenser for pens & cosmetics

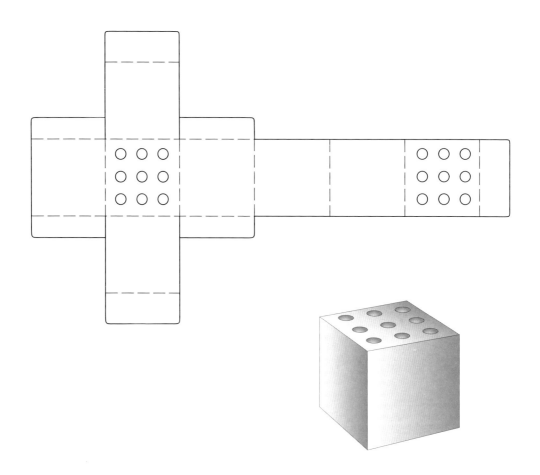

Two piece tower shaped POP

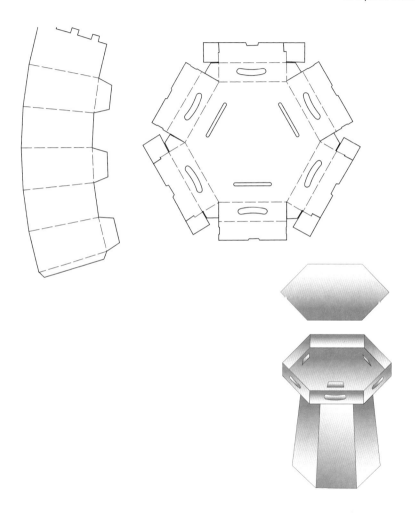

Two pieces slotted POP

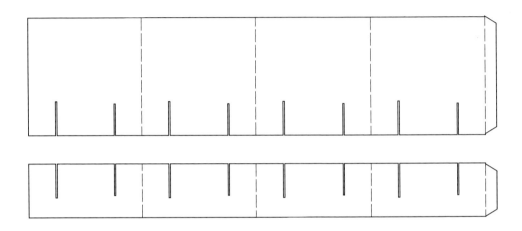

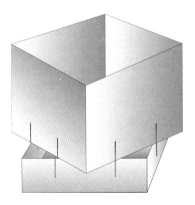

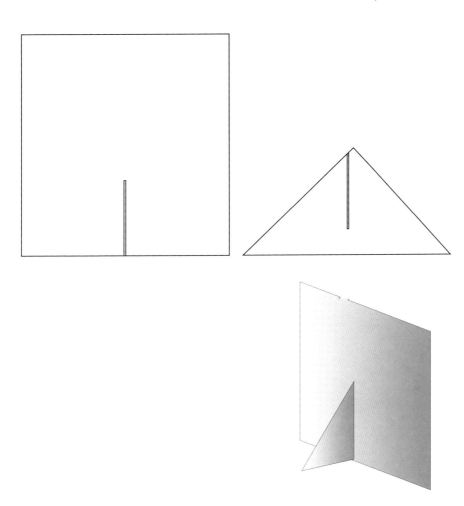

Two pieces slotted POP variation

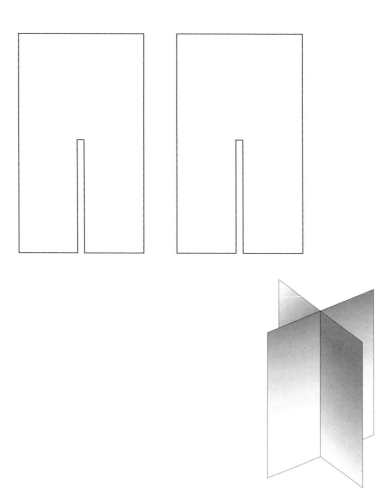

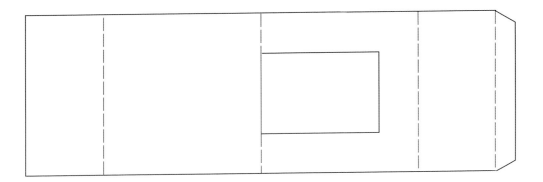

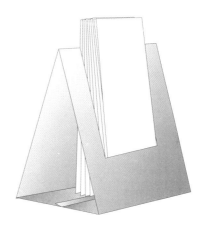

POP with backlock support

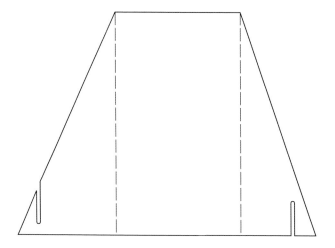

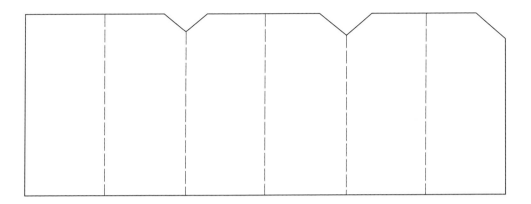

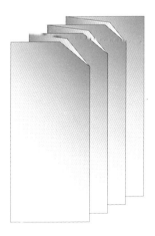

Folder type display

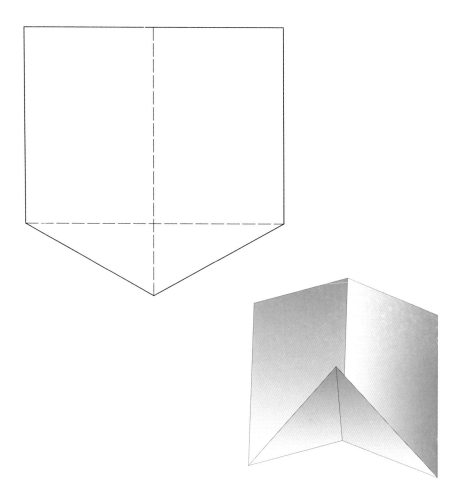

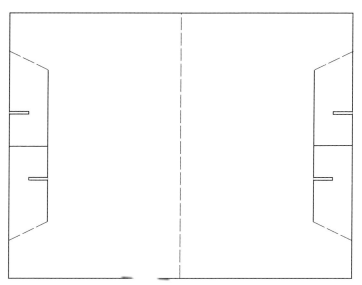

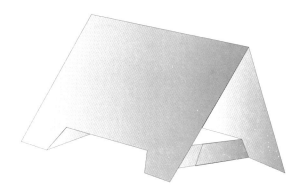

Roof type Two pieces display

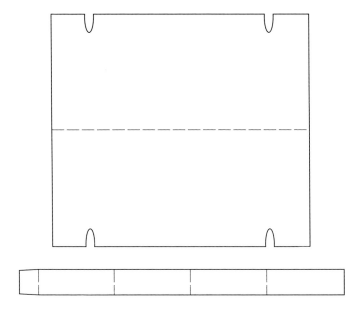

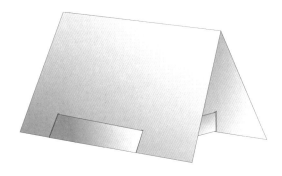

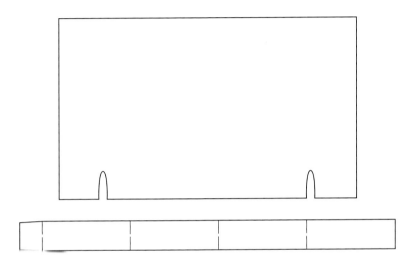

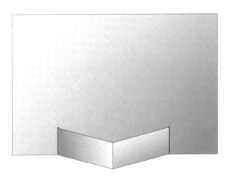

Centre locking display

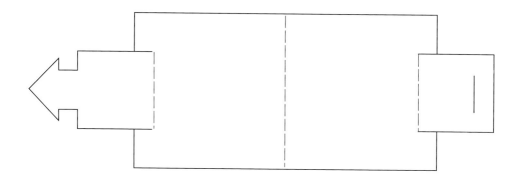

Single piece double wall Piramid shaped display

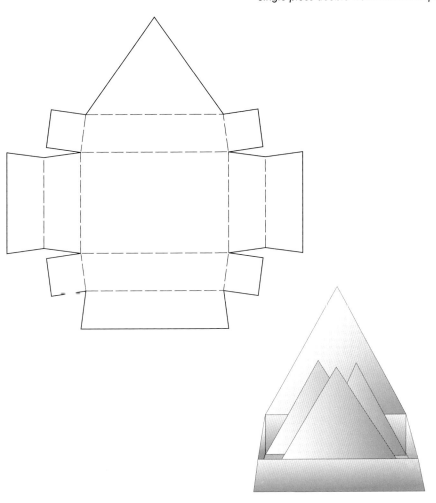

Gravity-fed dispenser with stand

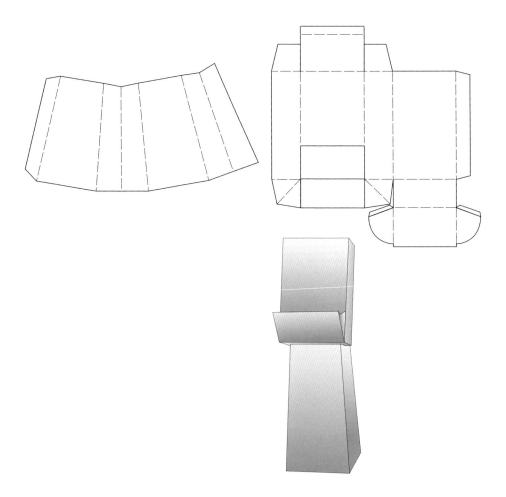

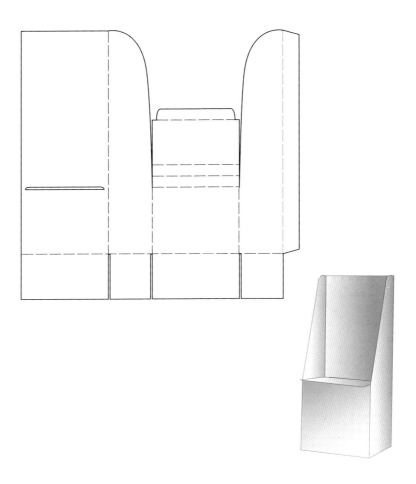

Single piece tapered sides display

10ft. high gate display for exhibition

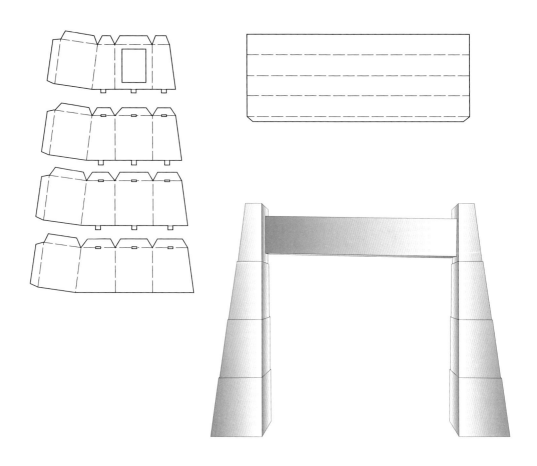

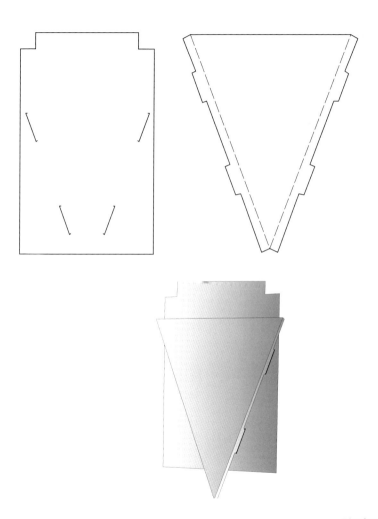

Three pieces pillor type display

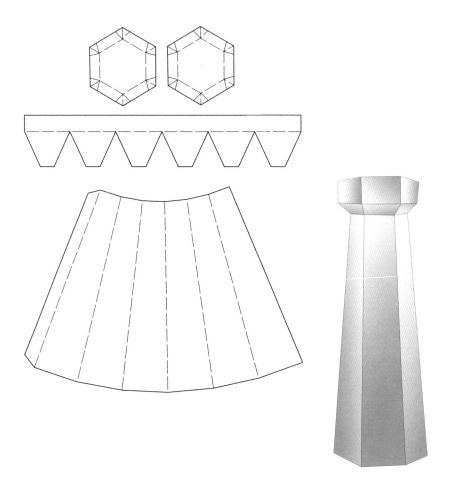

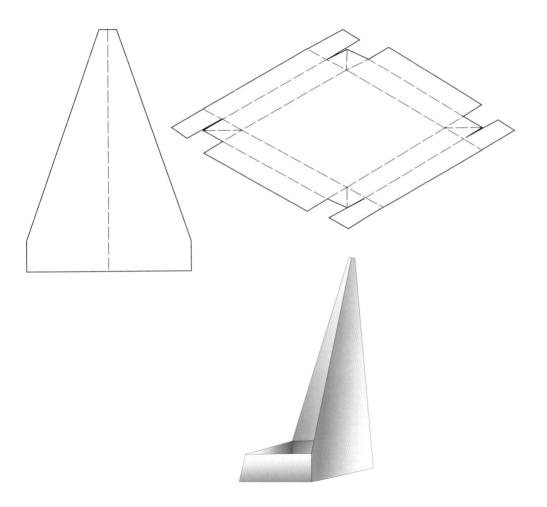

Floor display

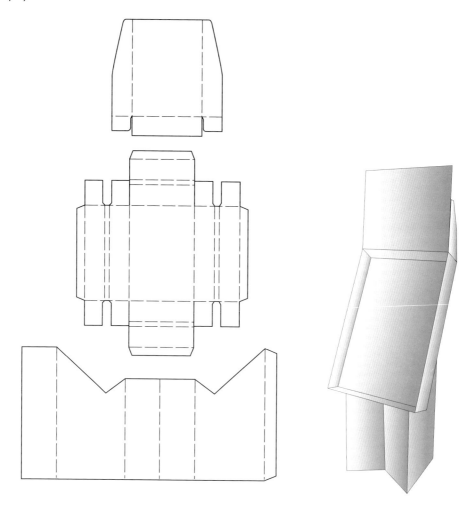

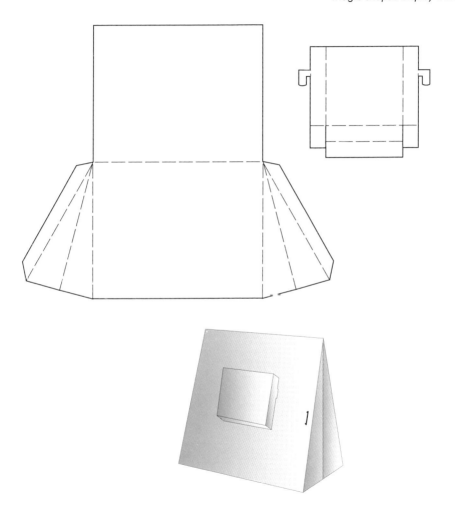

Display with backdrop

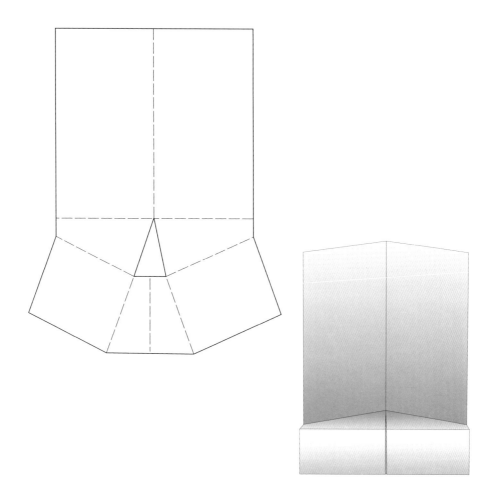

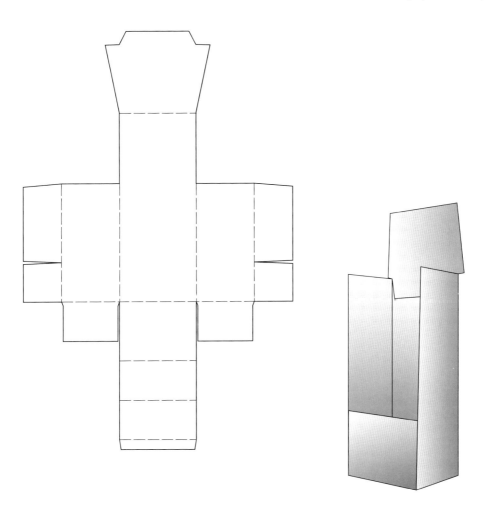

Floor Display with tear-open top

Single piece display with steps & backdrop

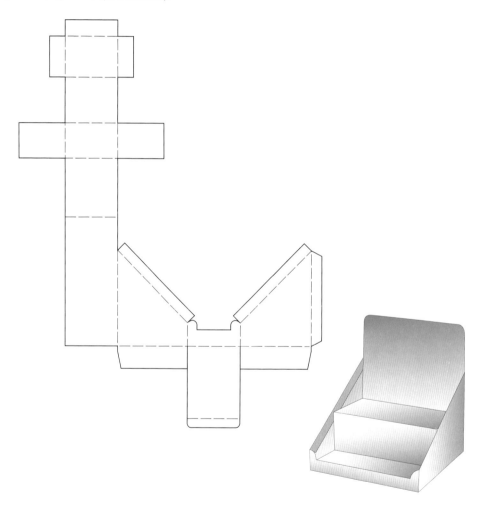

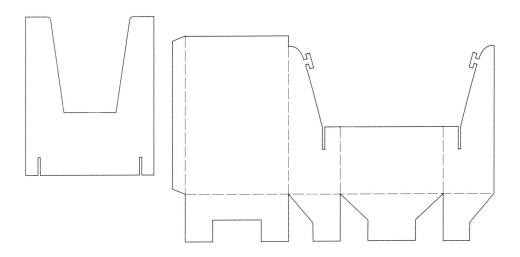

Auto assemble Foor Display

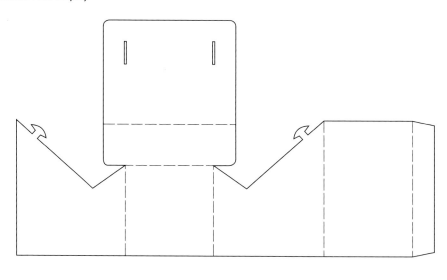

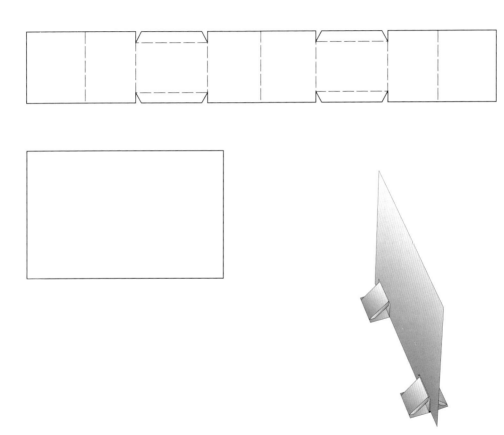

Hanging dispenser

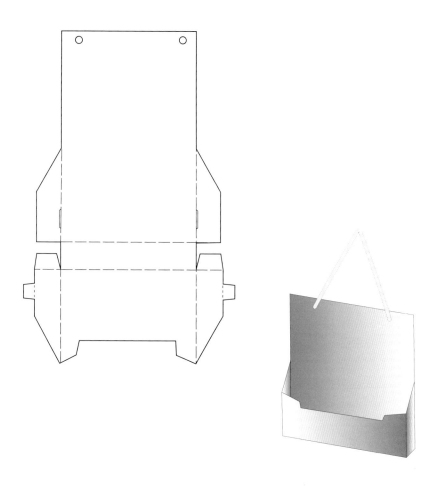

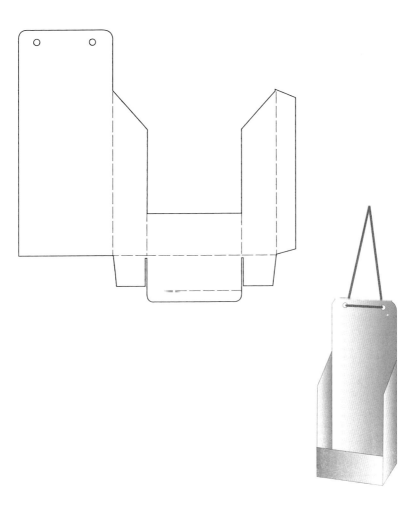

Hanging display with partition

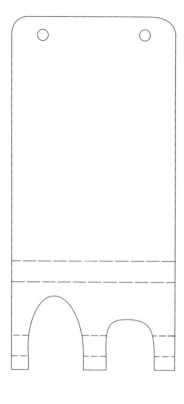

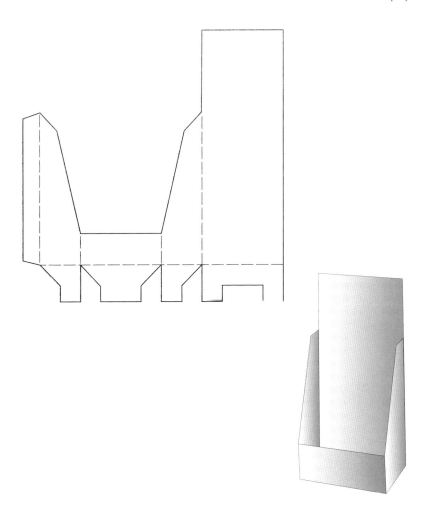

Three panel display with back pasting flap

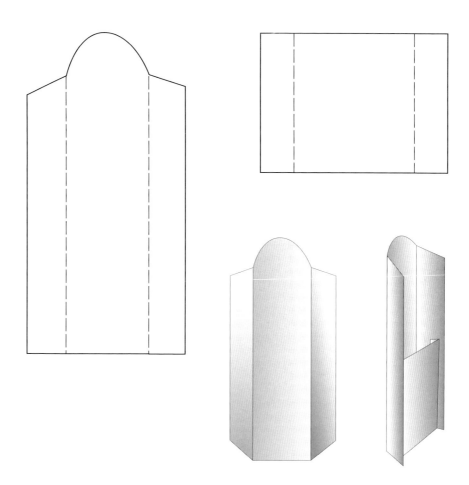

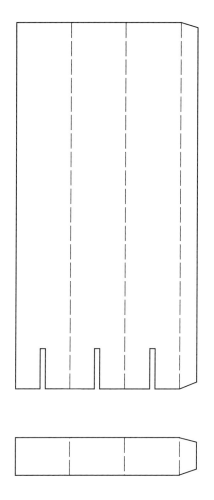

Pillor shaped display

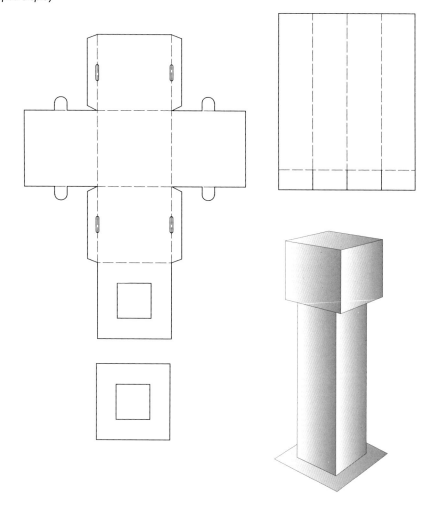

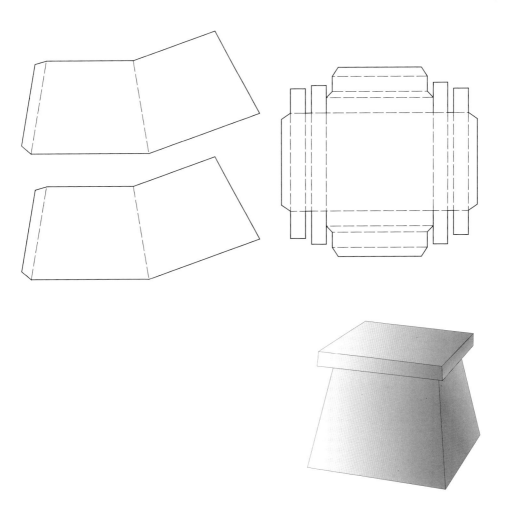

Tapered platform with hinged backdrop

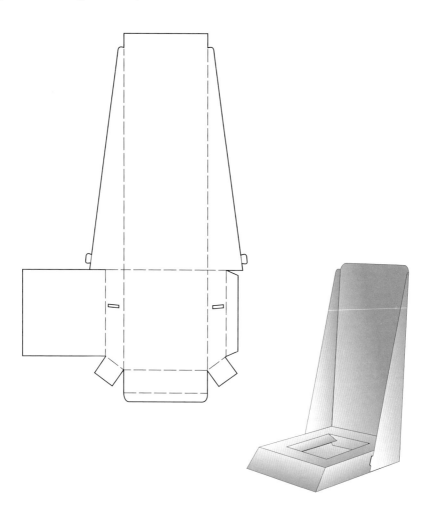

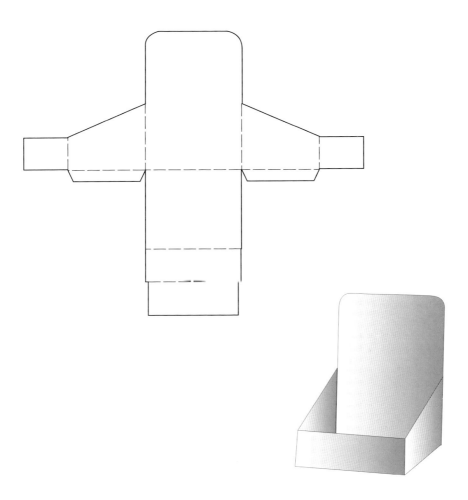

Single piece counter display

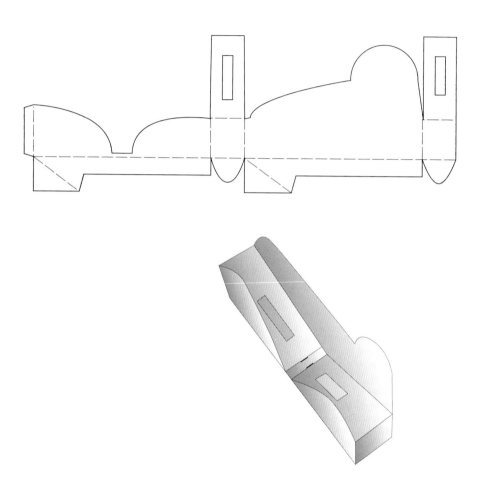

Curved display with tapered autolock backdrop

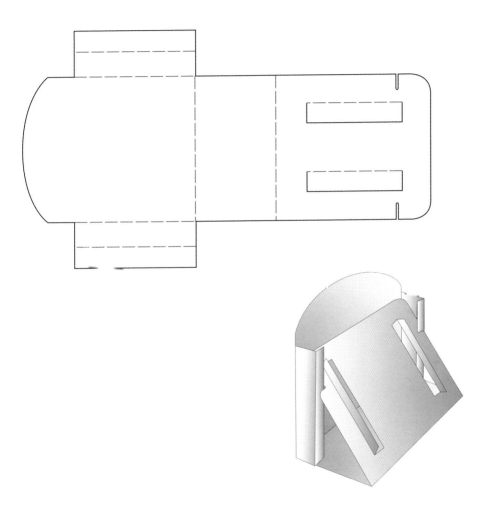

Curved display with tapered autolock backdrop variation

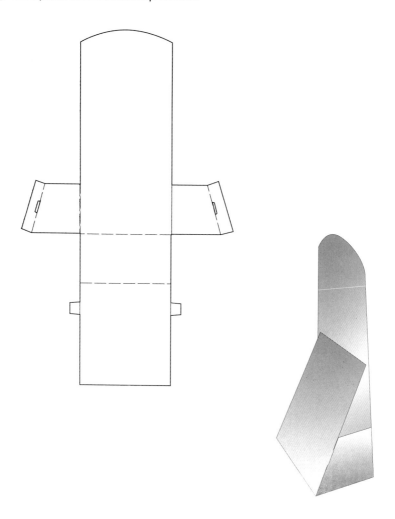

Tapered autolock display with hinged backdrop

Counter Display with Backdrop

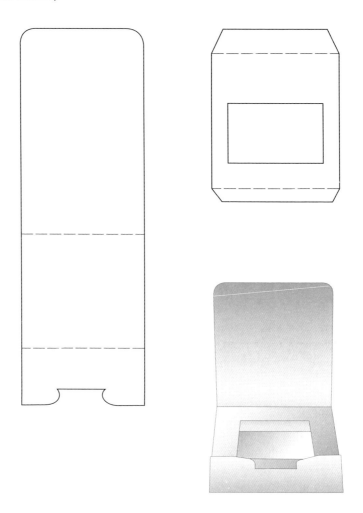

Two sides tapered display for pen

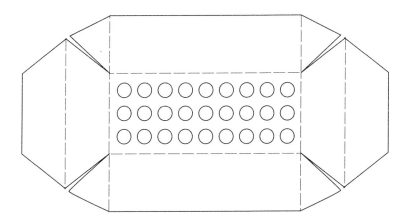

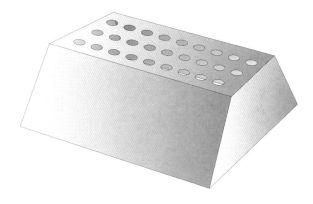

Tapered display with window

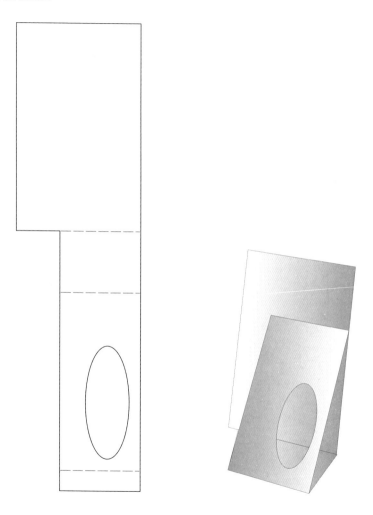

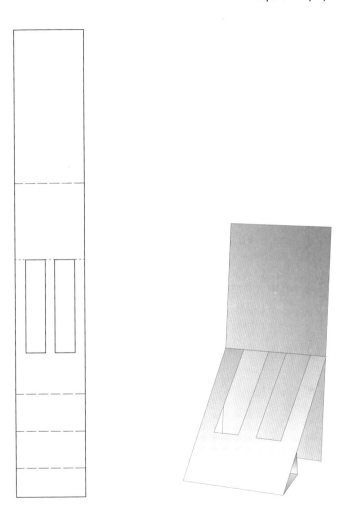

Triangle shaped display with centre locking

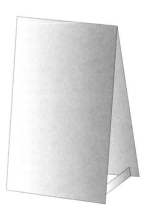

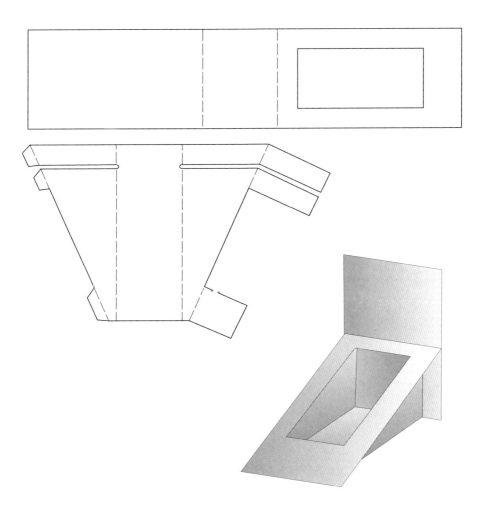

Hinged top with built in partition

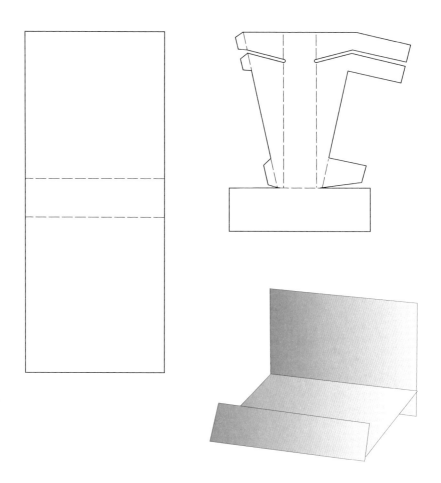

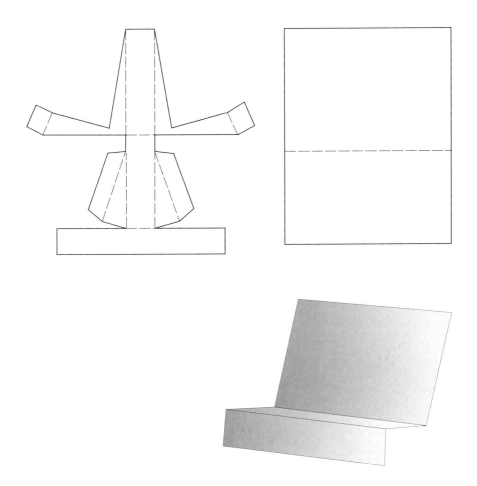

Wall hanging POP danglar Wall

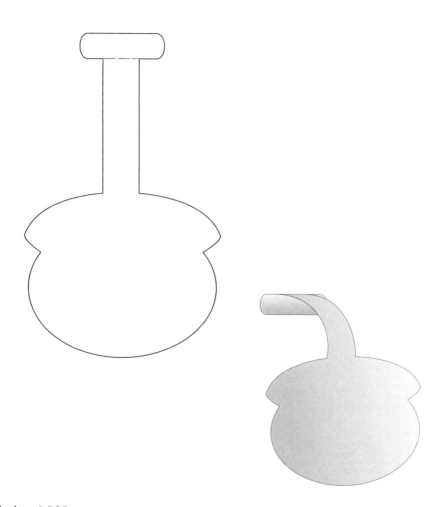

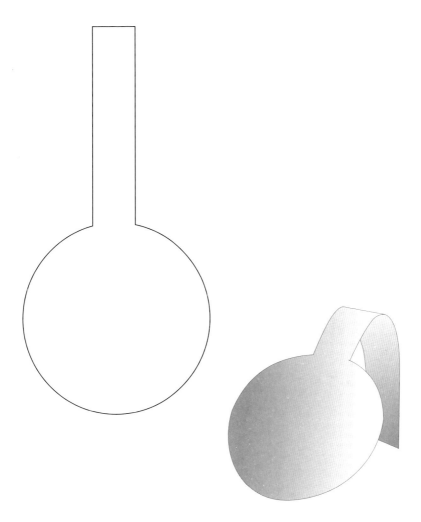

Counter display

Reverse tuck platform with forth backdrop panel

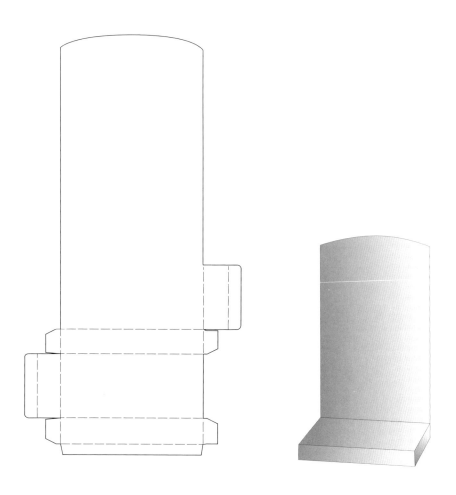

Single piece double pasting platform with hinged backdrop

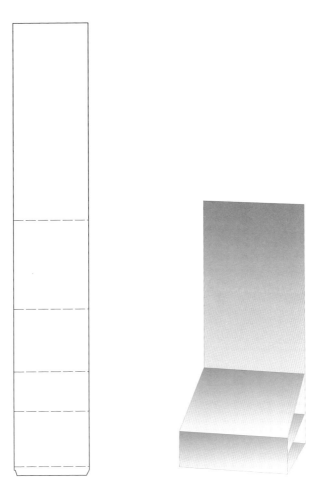

Floor display with slotted lock back support

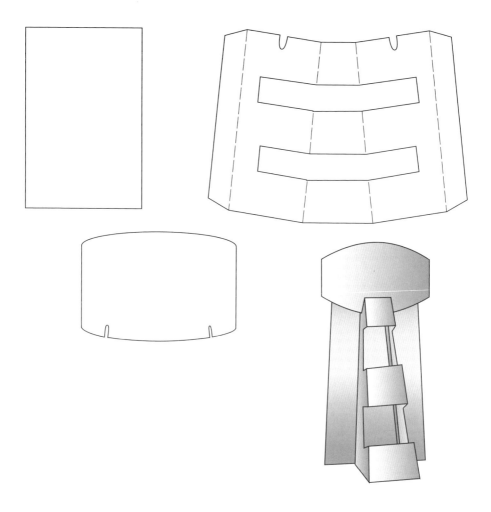

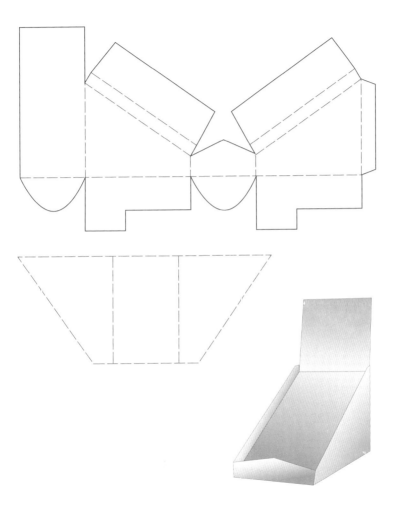

Vertical display with tuck lock backdrop

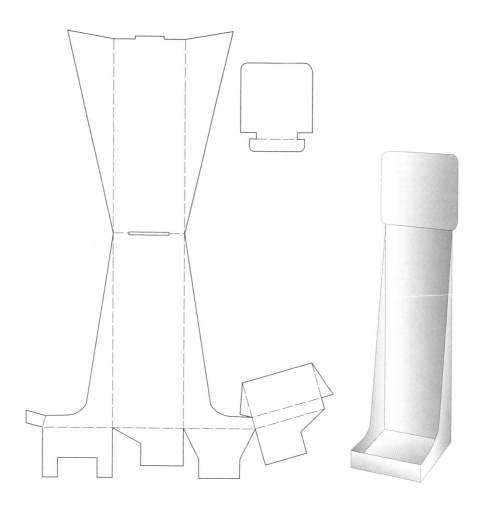

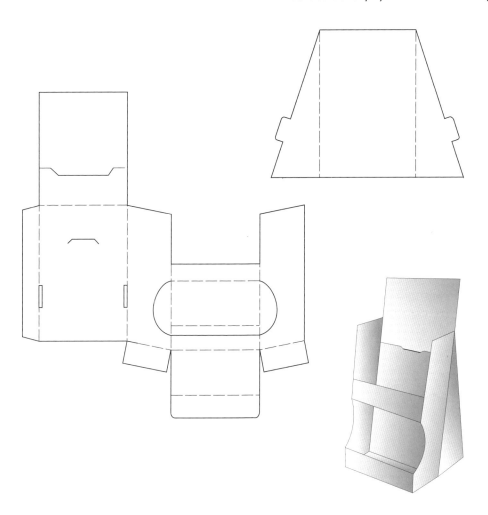

Center Table with display selves

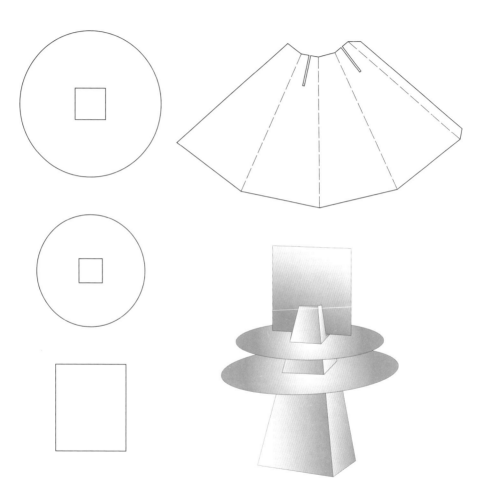

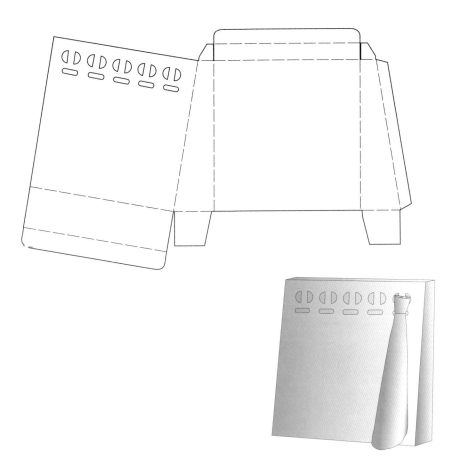

Pop-up Counter Display

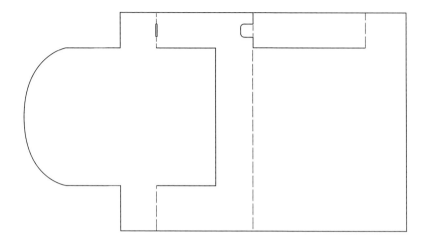

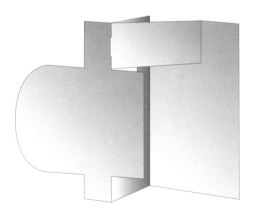

Tapered top display with separate double wall partitions

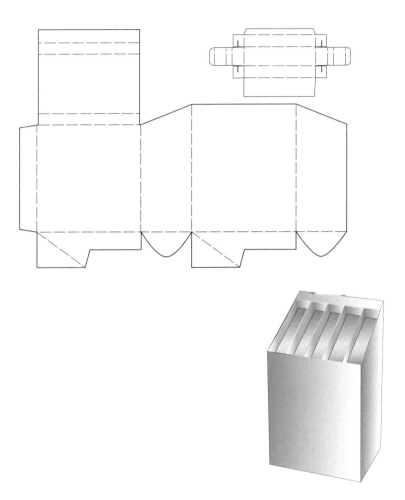

6 sides auto lock bottom outer with inner 6 sides supporter & slotted partitions

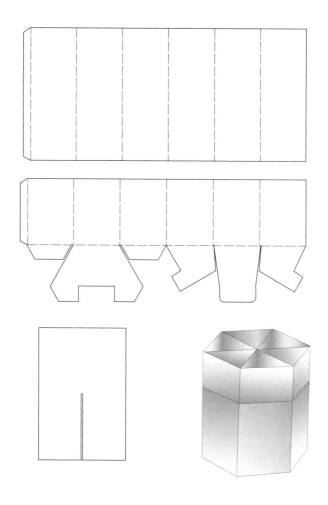

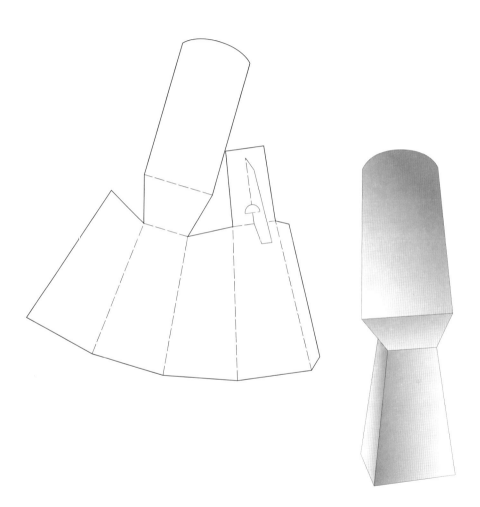

Tuck in flap bottom with curved end sides

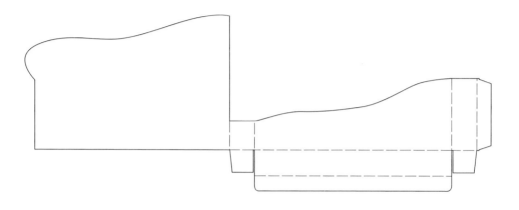

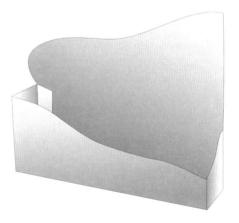

JACKETS

Wrap around pouch with interlocking flaps

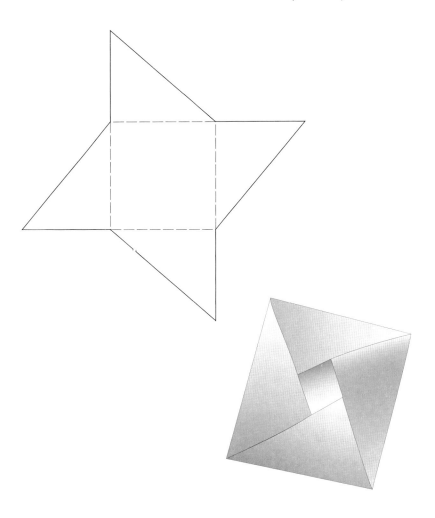

Single piece portfolio type jacket

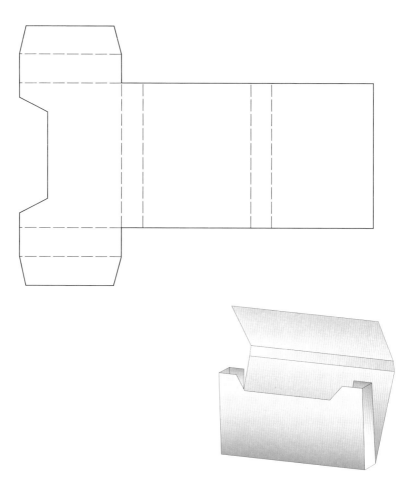

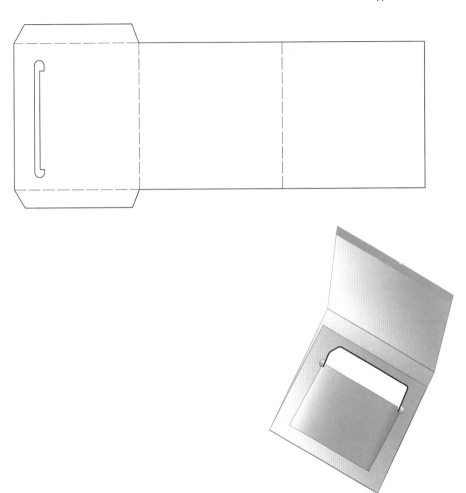

Jacket with Pasted pocket on right side & diary on left side

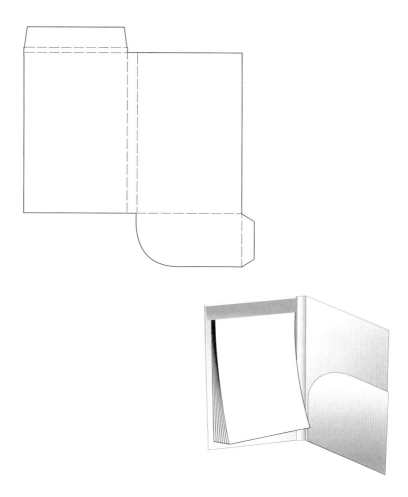

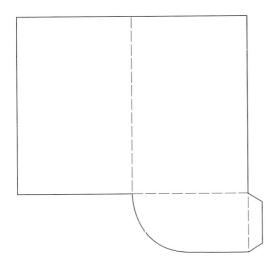

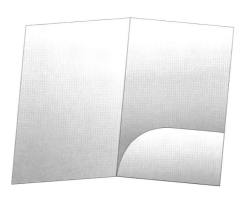

Single piece three fold jacket withdust flap & tuck-in flap

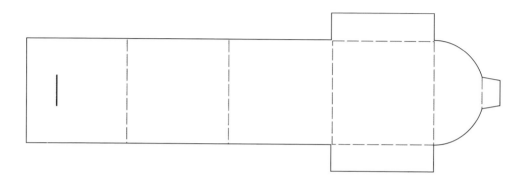

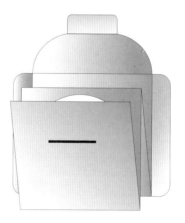

A jacket with pasted window pocket

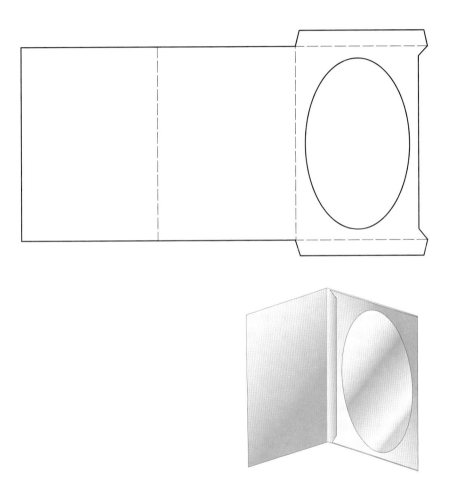

Three fold jacket with pasted pockets on two sides & one on center

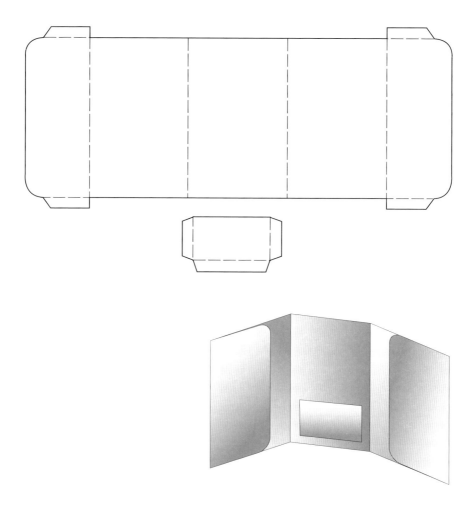

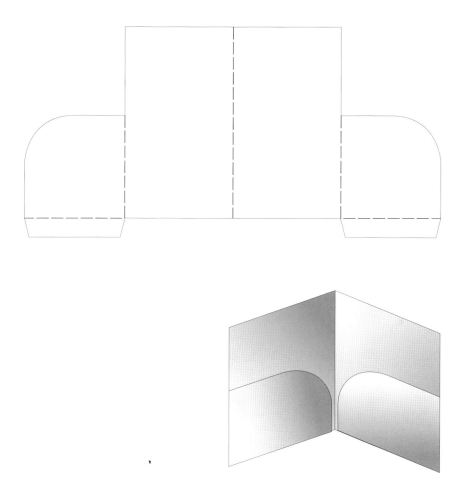

Jacket for digital CD

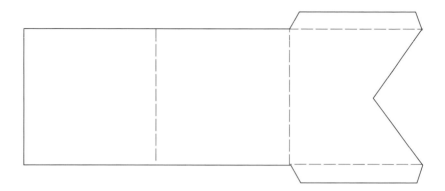

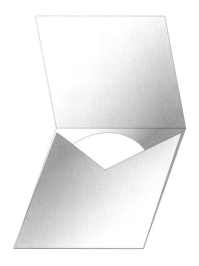

A CD jacket with triangle shape sides formating top

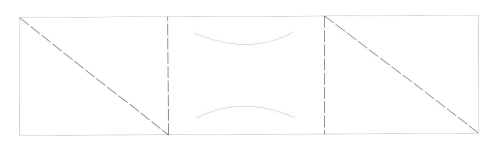

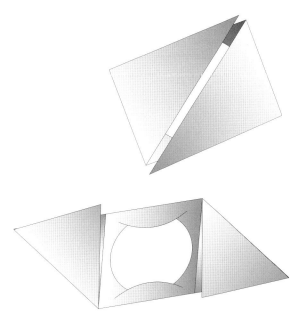

Three fold jacket for digital CD

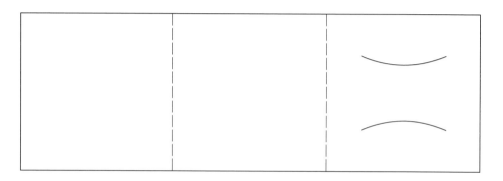

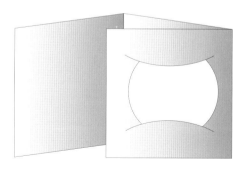

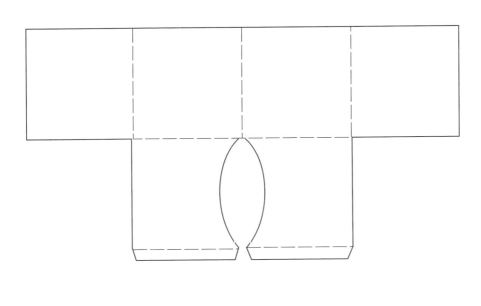

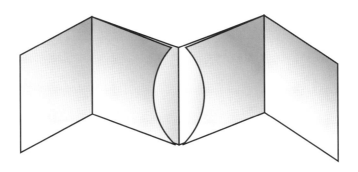

Jackets 257

CD Jacket variation

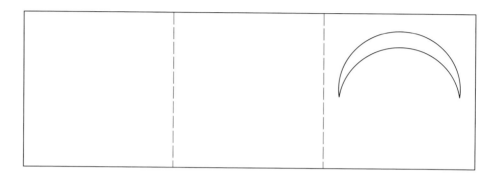

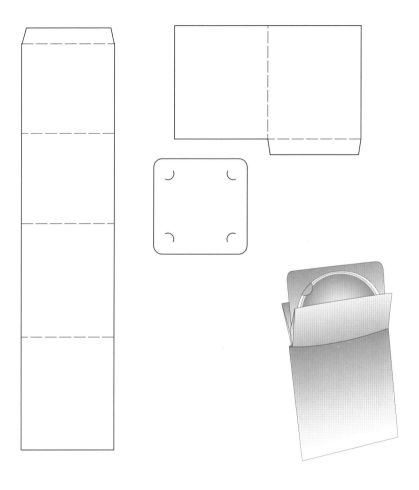

Multiple CD holder case

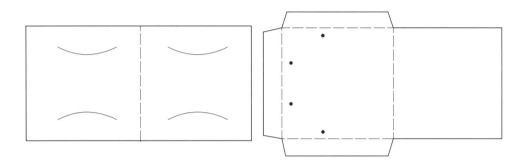

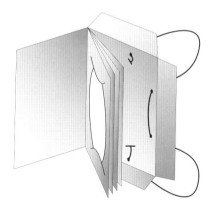

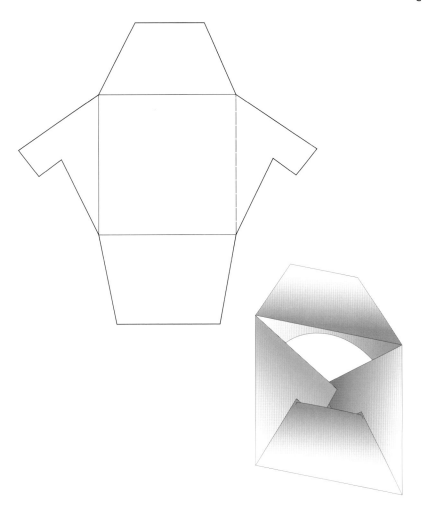

Folder type Six CD Holder

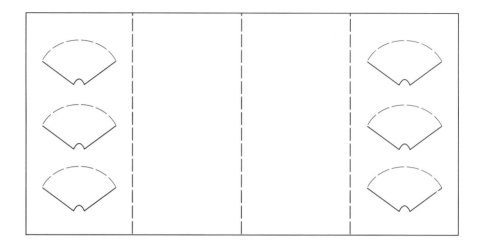

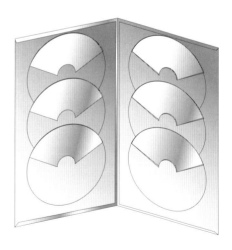

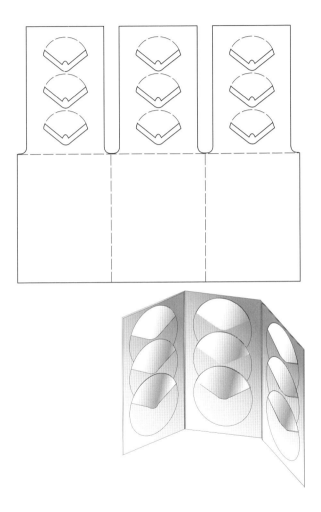

FILES & FOLDERS

Spiral bound book type folder

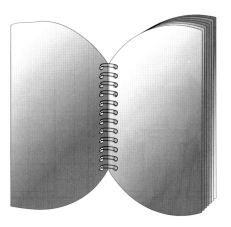

Bound Sample Holder

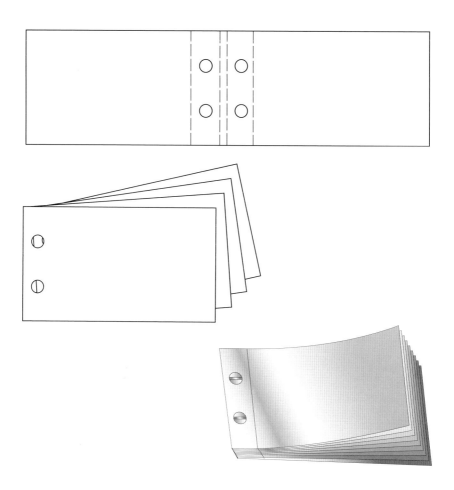

Telescopic type tray/lid Document Holder with window

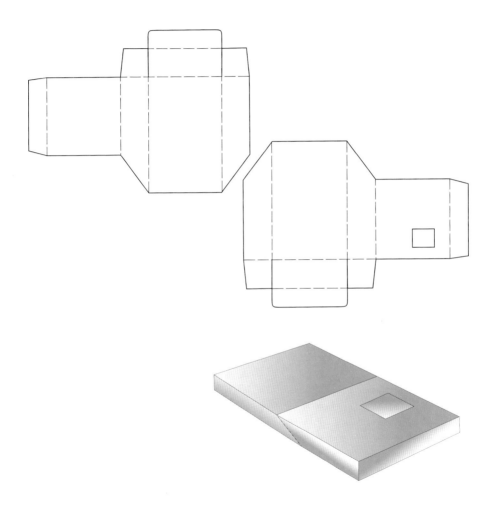

Spiral bounded curved shaped package

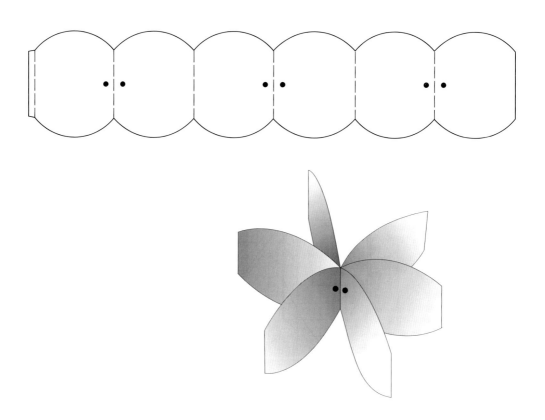

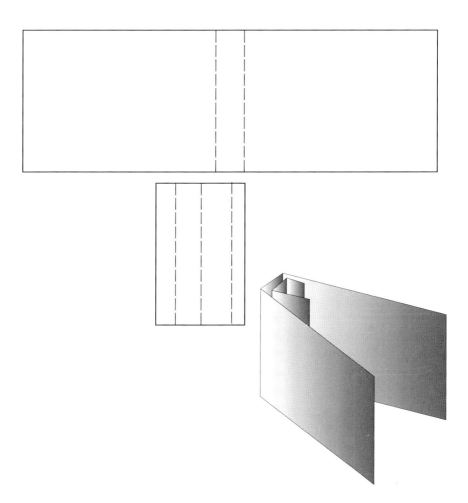

Three fold file with pasted pockets

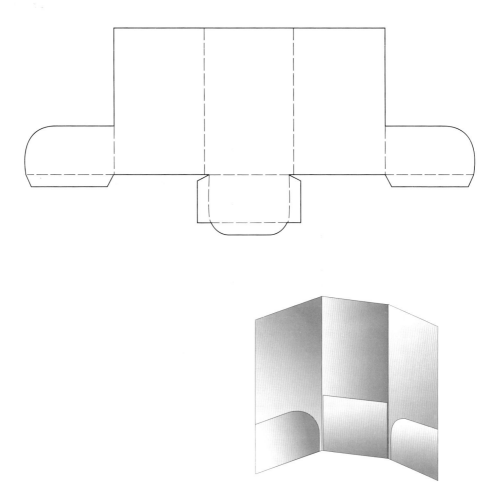

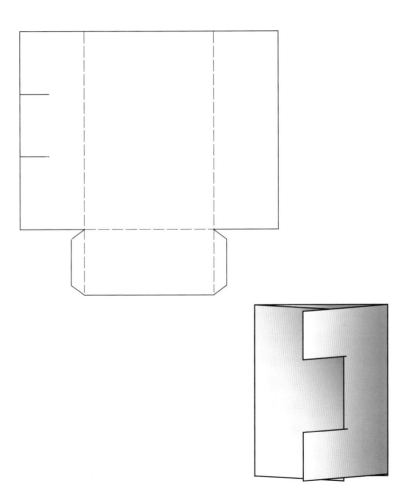

Document folder with four wall & locking flaps

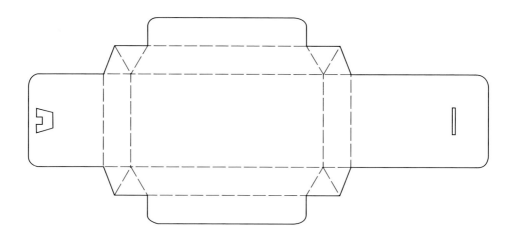

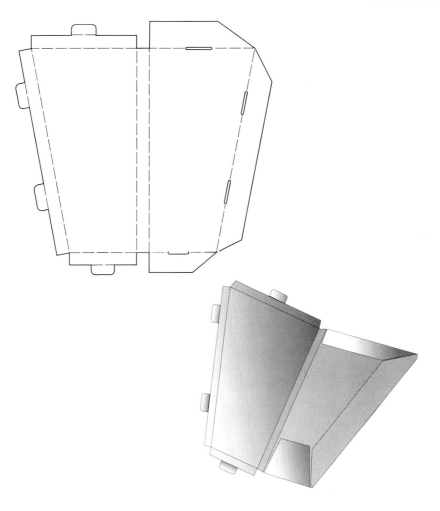

Eight Page Folder

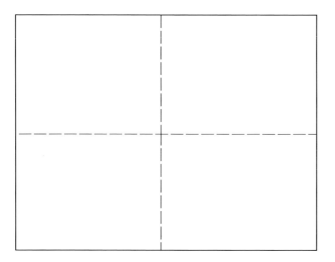

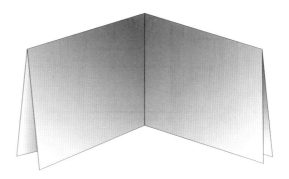

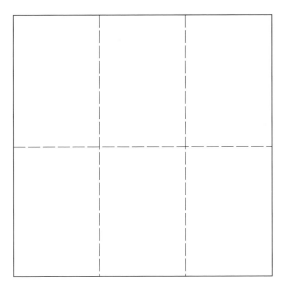

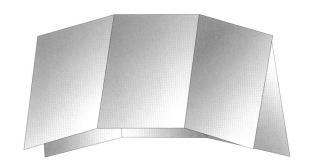

Twelve Page Accordion Folder

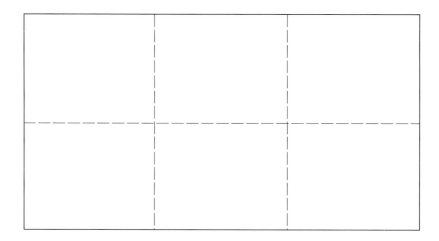

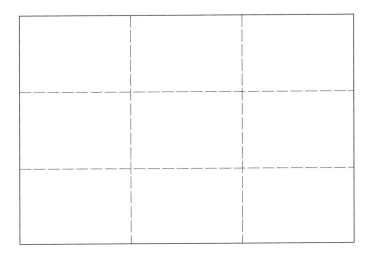

Eighteen Page Folder

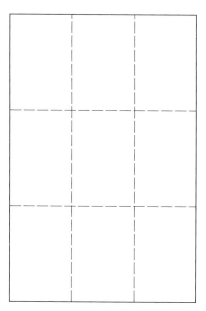

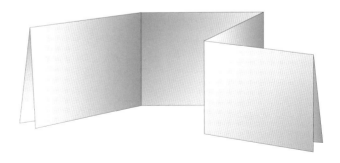

Forty Page Folder

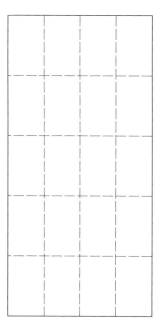

Forteen Page Accordion Folder

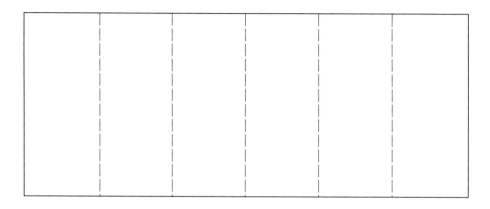

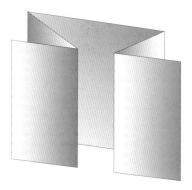

Gatefold with Tumb Index

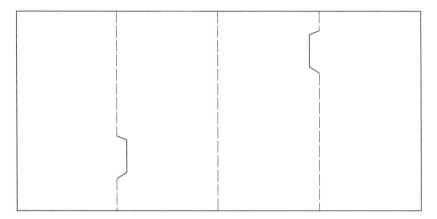

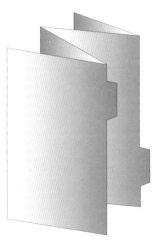

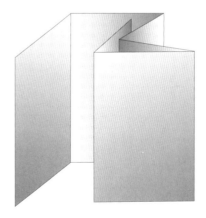

Variation Sixteen Page Folder

Variation Twenty Page Folder

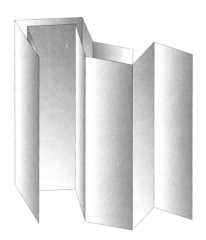

BAGS

Bag with tapered sides & holes for hanging belts

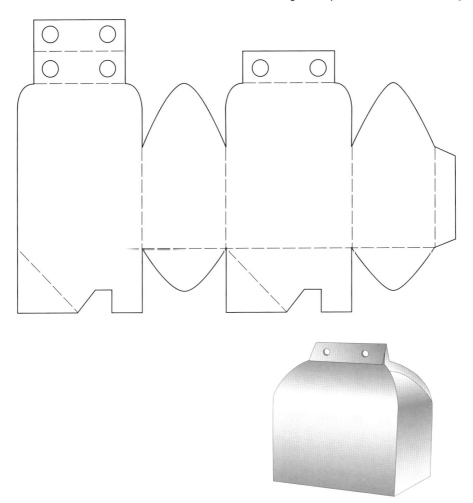

Bag with in built handles

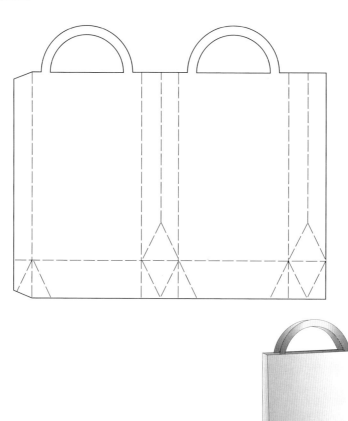

Bag with tapered curved sides &in built handles

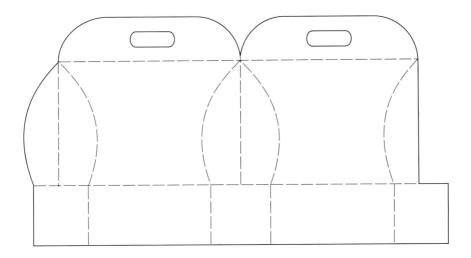

Sealable type Bags

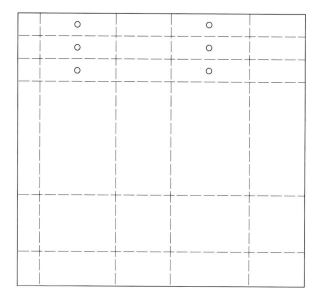

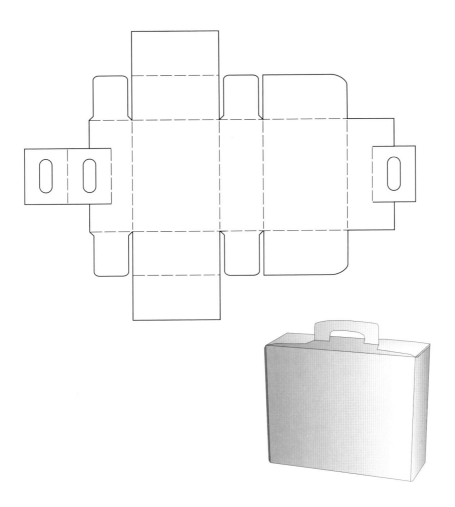

Grocery Bag

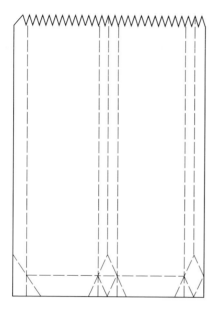

Self locking triangle shape bag with in built handles

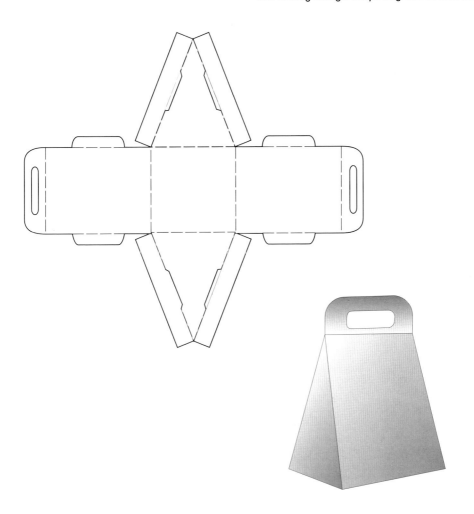

Pillow type T-shirt shaped bag

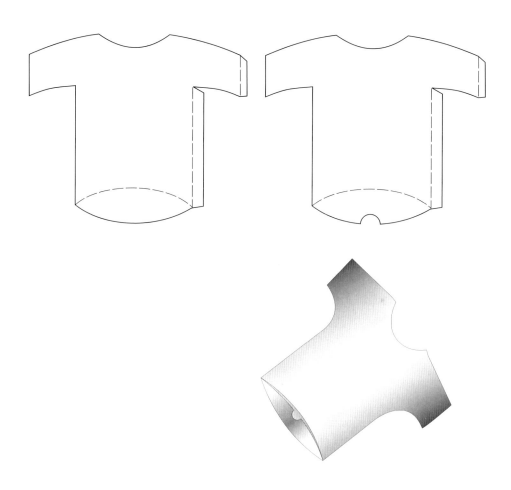

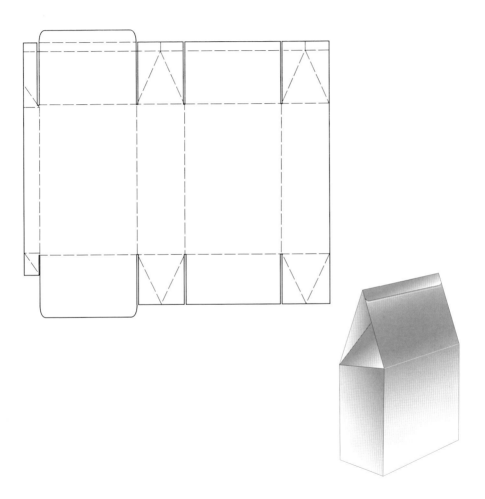

Two piece bag with inter locks & in built handles

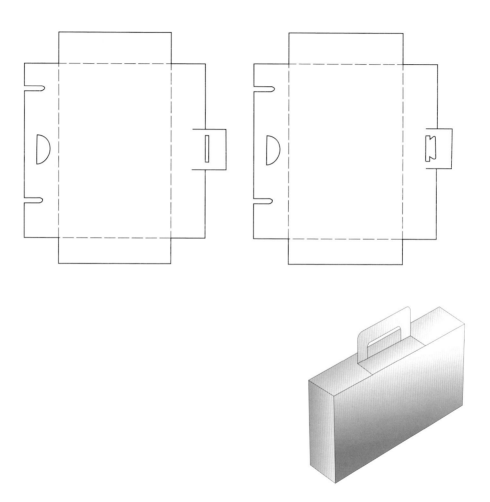

Box type bag with curved top & holes for hanging belts

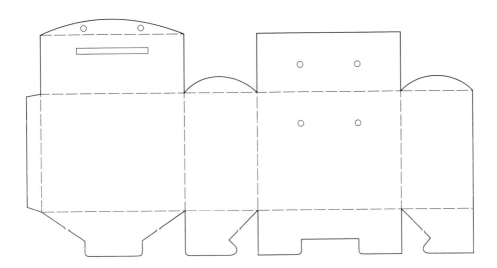

Bottom pasted bag with in built handle

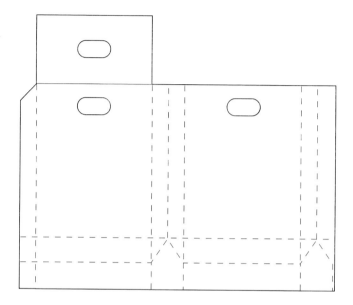

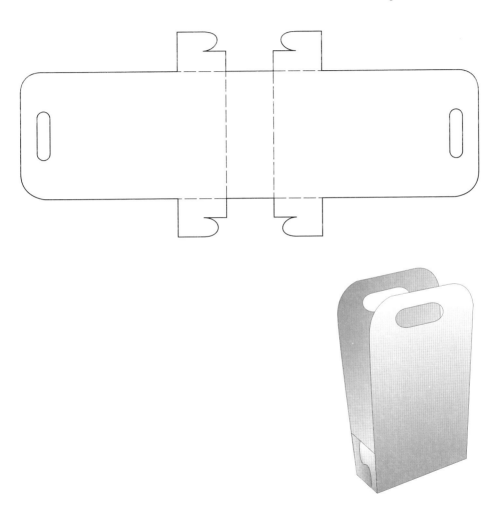

Interlocking sides with in built handles

Portfolio type bag with handle

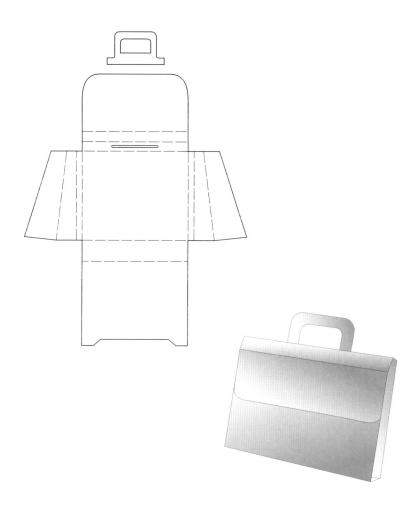

Bottom pasting triangle shape bag with holes for hanging belts

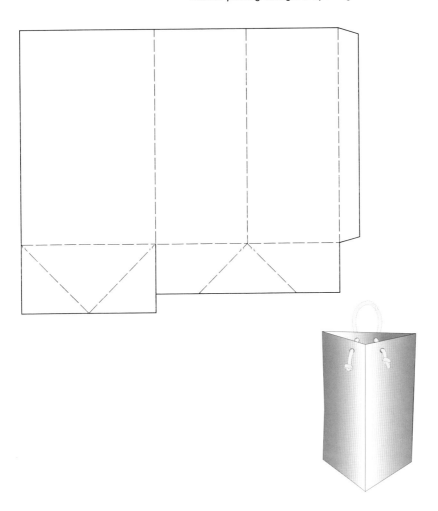